Shechinah, Bring Me Home!

Shechinah, Bring Me Home!

Kabbalah and the Omer in Real Life

Laura Duhan-Kaplan

CASCADE *Books* · Eugene, Oregon

SHECHINAH, BRING ME HOME!
Kabbalah and the Omer in Real Life

Cascade Books
An Imprint of Wipf and Stock Publishers
199 W. 8th Ave., Suite 3
Eugene, OR 97401

www.wipfandstock.com

PAPERBACK ISBN: 978-1-6667-4186-5
HARDCOVER ISBN: 978-1-6667-4187-2
EBOOK ISBN: 978-1-6667-4188-9

Cataloguing-in-Publication data:

Names: Duhan-Kaplan, Laura [author].

Title: Shechinah, bring me home! : Kabbalah and the Omer in real life / by Laura Duhan-Kaplan.

Description: Eugene, OR: Cascade Books, 2022 | Includes bibliographical references.

Identifiers: ISBN 978-1-6667-4186-5 (paperback) | ISBN 978-1-6667-4187-2 (hardcover) | ISBN 978-1-6667-4188-9 (ebook)

Subjects: LCSH: Cabala | Sefirah period | Meditation—Jewish | Mysticism—Judaism

Classification: BM525 number 2022 (print) | BM525 (ebook)

09/19/22

For Koi

and

his little sister

Keely

As the Holy One of Blessing fills the whole world,
so also does the soul fill the whole body.

As the Holy One of Blessing sees and is not seen,
so also the soul sees and is not seen.

As the Holy One of Blessing sustains the world,
so also does the soul sustain the body.

As the Holy One of Blessing is pure, so also is
the soul pure.

As the Holy One of Blessing dwells in the innermost chambers, so also does the soul dwell
in the innermost chambers.

Let the one who has these five things come and
praise the One who has these five things.

—*Babylonian Talmud, Berachot 10a, adapted*

Contents

Acknowledgements

How does a book become what it is? As the philosopher Aristotle said, "it's complicated." You get a creative spark, find some raw material, give it a shape, and hope an audience will find it useful.[1]

The creative spark came from Leslee Brown, director of Mind Body Passport adult learning programs. She invited me to co-teach a four-session webinar on Jung and Kabbalah. Together, we taught history, theory, and practice—including the 49-day *Sefirat ha'Omer* practice. As I touted it to the students, I realized: I need to take my own practice seriously this year.

Some of the raw material comes from great historical scholars, and I cite them throughout the book. But a series of great contemporary teachers brought the ideas alive for me, through discussion and application. In particular, I am grateful to Judith Z. Abrams, Lionel Corbett, Diane P. Freedman, Elliot Ginsberg, Miles Krassen, Alfred Louch, Gail Lyons, Daniel C. Matt, Harry O. Maier, Leah Novick, Marcia Prager, Judith Presler, John C. Reeves, Zalman Schachter-Shalomi, Daniel Siegel, Hanna Tiferet Siegel, Jennifer Selig, Bonnelle Strickling, and Chuck Young.

Some of the raw material comes from the life of my family. So I thank my husband Charles Kaplan, children Hillary Kaplan and

---

1. Technically, scholars say Aristotle spoke of four causes, material, formal, final, and efficient. Aristotle, *Metaphysics* 993a–995a.

Eli Kaplan, brother David Duhan, late mother Ruthie Duhan, late father Bernard Duhan, and late Aunt Sylvia Spector.

At first, the material took shape as a series of blog posts. In preparing the book, I honored that shape, with some editing, of course. I also added an introduction to *Sefirat ha'Omer*. Several scholars helped me trace the documentation of early ideas and practices. For this, I thank T'mimah Ickovitz, Pinchas Giller, Justin Goldstein, and Eugene Fleischman Sotirescu. Editors at Wipf & Stock made it possible to turn the manuscript into a book. I thank George Callihan and Matthew Wimer for their careful work, and Robin Parry for his thoughtful, collegial work.

There was an audience who found the original posts useful. Several hundred people followed the blog series. Many commented regularly, engaging personally with the ideas and stories. For this, I thank Dael Adams, Mary Adlersberg, Elana Brief, Jacquelyn Contreras, Julie Hilton Danan, David Duhan, Elizabeth, Michal Mivasair Fox, Howard Goldman, Frieda Gramit, David Hepler, Elaine M. Hyman, Evan J. Krame, Julie Leavitt, Faith Leonard, Harriett Lemer, Robert Lewis, Colleen Lissamer, Lynda, Shira Macklin, Lorilee Mallek, Mati, Goldie Milgram, Chava Monastersky, Linda Mulhall, Yael Raff Peskin, Katharine Proudlove, Marianne Rev, Robert, Anita Rosenfield, Wendy Rubin, Jennifer Sharlow, Jessica Shimberg, Karen Soria, Susan Swanson, Meg Watson, Ellen Weaver, Twilla Tiferet Welch, Rebecca Woodland, Cheratra Yaswen, and Rain Zohav.

Among those offering comments, one stands out in particular: my husband Charles Kaplan, who travelled the Omer journey with me, reading drafts, discussing ideas, feeling feelings, and reviewing our life together. Thank you, Chas.

Laura Duhan-Kaplan

Vancouver, BC

Traditional, ancestral, and unceded territories of the
Musqueam, Squamish, and Tsleil-Waututh Peoples

Kabbalah That Counts

Sefirat Ha'Omer and the
Journey of Shechinah

T his is and is not a timeless book.

Sure, I talk about some timeless ideas, like "wisdom," "beauty," "eternity," and "cosmic mother." I explore them using the Kabbalistic version of an old Jewish spiritual practice called *Sefirat ha'Omer.* This forty-nine-day meditation program helps us see how spiritual qualities move inside our own thoughts and feelings. So, it turns us towards big ideas but also towards the details of our lives. And those specific details of time and place are important, too. This book, in fact, is full of them.

I live on Sophia Street, in a trendy urban neighborhood. Here, small one-family homes crowd close together, separated only by old trees and thick hedges. Crows, ravens, woodpeckers, and songbirds fill the landscape. So do raccoons, skunks, squirrels, rats, and the occasional coyote. Nearby, there's a Main Street lined with late-night bars and eateries.

Early one morning, I heard a neighbor yell. "F***ing moron. You f***ing moron. You're a f***ing moron."

But there was no argument. No fighting back. No second voice at all.

Maybe he was yelling at a badly parked car. Or at whoever left a pile of garbage on his lawn. Maybe he was even yelling at himself.

Later that day, I heard a teenage neighbor wail. "No, mom!" she cried. "It's an animal."

"We have to kill it," said the mom. She was loud and firm. Matter-of-fact.

"No, mom! It's still an animal."

I couldn't see them and they couldn't see me. Still, I walked towards the hedge that separates our homes. "Whatever it is, throw it in our yard."

At least, that's what I planned to say. But before I could speak, the daughter howled, "No no no no no no nooooo!" And I knew it was over.

I have no idea what they killed. Maybe it was a poisonous spider or a snake. Or a rat, already dazed by their dog. But whatever it was, I still can't get their voices out of my head.

Later that same night, I heard a young man shout. "Get out of the road, a**hole! What's wrong with you!"

I stuck my head out the window. I saw two burly men in a car and one slender man standing on the curb. He seemed a bit tipsy; clearly he had just staggered across the road. Now he was typing on his phone, probably texting a friend to pick him up.

But the driver was still upset that he had nearly hit a pedestrian. He may have been tipsy himself, heading home from a Main Street bar. So he continued to berate the man on the curb—the one he had almost killed.

Then the driver got an idea. "Come here," he called. The more drunken man stepped off the curb and approached the car. "Show me your wallet," the driver said. So the drunk put his hand in his pocket.

"Come on, guys!" I yelled in my *I-am-a-grandma-so-WTF-is-this* voice.

Caught and shamed, the driver started his car and left. I looked around for the drunk, but he had fled, too.

Let's face it: screaming at yourself, killing a harmless animal, and stealing from a drunk are *not good things*. They are clues that people are unraveling and our social fabric is fraying. And that the world is in need of *tikkun,* repair, as we say in the jargon of Kabbalah.

You know, I'm not really a grandmother.[1] But I've raised my children and buried my parents, so these guys in the street looked pretty young to me. And, believe me, they recognized "the voice" when they heard it. Not my voice, but their own mother's voice, inside them. But why should I be surprised? Kabbalah teaches that *tikkun* rests on finding our inner mother, and healing our relationship with her. In fact, Kabbalah calls that mother *Shechinah,* the indwelling presence of God.[2] And it designates a specific season for this healing, the season of *Sefirat ha'Omer.*

In this book, I invite you to join me on one of my annual journeys towards *Shechinah.* But first, I'd like to take you on a quick tour of the history of Kabbalah. It will help you to understand more deeply the ideas behind this deeply personal book. I'll talk about Kabbalah's philosophical foundations, its allegorical way of reading Torah, and its approach to *Sefirat ha'Omer.* And then, I'll tell you how those ideas will thread through the main part of this book.

Kabbalah: Philosophical Foundations

The word Kabbalah literally means "tradition." In contemporary English, we call it a mystical tradition. Sometimes, we call it a philosophy, and that's not wrong.[3] Kabbalah does borrow from the ideas of the ancient Greek philosopher Plato. If you studied philosophy, you may remember Plato's famous "allegory of the cave." An allegory is a kind of parable. It tells a story that is just a little bit odd, in a way that points you to a deeper hidden meaning. Imagine, Plato says, prisoners chained to a bench in a dimly lit cave. They can look in only one direction, where they see shadows of artistic representations of reality. Suppose one prisoner breaks free, and leaves the cave. The sudden rush of sunlight blinds them.

1. Yet. No pressure, kids.
2. Tishby, *Wisdom of the Zohar,* vol 1, 371–87.
3. Drob, "Tzimtzum."

Gradually, their sight returns, but nothing looks familiar. They have to learn a new way of perceiving and interpreting.[4]

Do these prisoners really exist? Yes, says Plato, they do—*we* are the prisoners. We are trapped in a misleading version of reality. Our senses bring us constantly shifting information. Popular culture adds innuendo and rumor. So, our knowledge is unstable.[5] But we cling to it anyway, because we are materialists.[6] We chase wealth and fame, believing and repeating whatever it takes to get them. But perhaps we occasionally hear echoes of a deeper reality of ideas and ideals: goodness, justice, equality, and beauty.[7] And then, we expand our consciousness to grasp the true forms the Creator had in mind.[8]

The first-century Jewish philosopher Philo of Alexandria loved the dialogues of Plato, and he also loved the Torah of Moses. As Philo saw it, Plato and Moses were teachers on a single spiritual path.[9] Philo believed that Moses wrote the Torah as an extended allegory, encoding his philosophy in stories and laws.[10] Sometimes, Philo says, Moses writes in a deliberately puzzling way, to remind us to read allegorically. For example, Moses tells us that God creates the heavens and the earth. But the earth God creates isn't earth as we know it; instead, it is chaotic and empty. God creates light. But it's not light as we know it, since God has not yet created the sun. All our confusion disappears, Philo says, when we understand Moses' point. God first created a "heaven," a spiritual realm of ideas, and then used those ideas to structure a chaotic world of matter.[11] As the Torah continues, stories of ancestral heroes teach us how to live well in this material world.

4. Plato, *Republic* 514a–520a.
5. Plato, *Republic* 509d–510a.
6. Plato, *Phaedo* 81b.
7. Plato, *Phaedo* 74a–75d.
8. Plato, *Timaeus,* 27c–29d.
9. Philo, "On the Creation" 8.
10. Duhan-Kaplan, "Body and Soul."
11. Philo, "On the Creation" 16–22.

Abraham's war against the four kings, for example, teaches us to not let our senses rule us.[12]

Philosophy of the *Sefirot*

Philo's writing helps us understand the thirteenth-century *Zohar*, the classic anthology of Kabbalah. The *Zohar* is a kind of mystical novel about the adventures of second-century Rabbi Shimon bar Yochai and his students.[13] They wander the countryside, teaching allegorical interpretations of the Torah. The stories and laws all point to a deep structure of ten metaphysical ideas. The life of these ideas begins within the Infinite God *(Eyn Sof)*.[14] *Eyn Sof* emanates energy, in the form of light. The energy shapes itself into a series—subtle, intellectual, emotional, dense/enduring—of forms that interact to weave a template for the world.[15] The forms are called *sefirot*: sacred books, stories, and numbers rolled into one.[16] The *sefirot* are more lively than Plato's or Philo's ideas; the *sefirot* sparkle with creative and procreative energy. Some, such as understanding *(binah)* and presence *(Shechinah)*, are motherly; others, including wisdom *(chochmah)* and splendor *(tiferet)*, are fatherly.[17] They come together in the Great Parent of the universe: an infinite, dynamic integration of male and female qualities, that births and sustain everything.

Here is a traditional diagram of the *sefirot*.[18] Look at it carefully. Take note of the names of the *sefirot* and their order. Notice, as well, the shape of the diagram. Some say it looks like a human

---

12. Philo, "On Abraham" 164–65.

13. Matt (tr.), *Zohar*, Vol. 1, xvii.

14. *Tikkunei Zohar*, 70:122b, 57:91b.

15. *Zohar*, 1:15a. The series is called in Hebrew *seder hishtalshelut*, the chain of emanation. See, for example, Schneerson, *True Existence*, 40.

16. *Sefer Yetzirah* 1:1.

17. Green, *Ehyeh*, Kindle.

18. The diagram is adapted from one drawn by Johann Reuchlin (1455–1522), which was first published on the cover of Gikatilla, *Gates of Light*.

body.[19] And, in fact, the *Zohar* says that the spiritual body—soul, psyche, or mind—of the first human being is made of *sefirot*.[20] Others say this image looks like a tree, perhaps like the Tree of Life planted in Eden at the origin of the world.[21] The fruit of the tree is the wisdom of Torah, correctly decoded with proper understanding of the *sefirot*.[22]

19. See, for example, *Tikkunei Zohar,* Second Introduction, 17a-b.

20. *Zohar* 3:170a.

21. Gen 2:9.

22. The argument that Torah is a tree of life is developed by a line connecting Prov 3:18, Ben Sira (Sir 24:23; 39:1), and *Zohar* 1:35a:8.

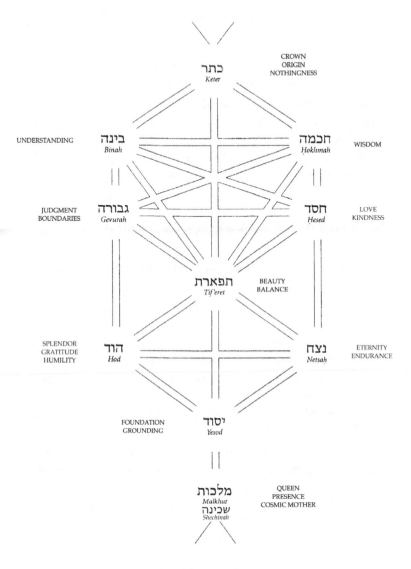

CROWN
ORIGIN
NOTHINGNESS

כתר
Keter

UNDERSTANDING
בינה
Binah

חכמה
Hokhmah
WISDOM

JUDGMENT
BOUNDARIES
גבורה
Gevurah

חסד
Hesed
LOVE
KINDNESS

תפארת
Tif'eret
BEAUTY
BALANCE

SPLENDOR
GRATITUDE
HUMILITY
הוד
Hod

נצח
Netsah
ETERNITY
ENDURANCE

FOUNDATION
GROUNDING
יסוד
Yesod

מלכות
Malkhut
שכינה
Shechinah
QUEEN
PRESENCE
COSMIC MOTHER

The Ten Sefirot

Torah as Mystical Allegory

The Torah, says the *Zohar*, is full of information about the divine parent. But to find it, you have to read stories and laws *allegorically*. Let's start with the creation of humanity. God says, "Let us create a human in our image."[23] But who is this "us"? Why, it is the ten *sefirot*, agreeing together to manifest in the human psyche.[24] Let's continue with an ancestral story. When Jacob meets Rachel, he rolls a heavy stone off the village well. Thus, he opens a romantic relationship that births the Jewish people.[25] But this is not just a human love story; it also tells us about the divine parent. When the masculine energy of *tiferet* allows the feminine energy of *Shechinah* to flow, the two together birth the world.[26]

And let's look at a ritual practice, too. The Torah introduces a yearly calendar of festivals. The first holiday is Passover, a seven-day celebration of the exodus. There's also a special agricultural ritual for the second day of Passover. Every grain farmer brings a sheaf *(omer)* of new grain to a priest, who lifts it up "in the presence of God."[27] The community then counts *(sefar)* seven weeks *(shavuot)*. On the fiftieth day, farmers bring freshly baked breaks and celebrate the harvest.[28] By the time the *Zohar* was written, the *Shavuot* festival was also a celebration of the revelation at Mt. Sinai—which, as Torah says elsewhere, happened approximately seven weeks after the Red Sea crossing.[29]

This seven-week ritual cycle, says the *Zohar*, tells a story about *Shechinah*. Even when the Israelites are enslaved, *Shechinah* is present with them as a kind of loving protector. When God liberates them, *Shechinah*, too, is liberated. And the Israelites,

23. Gen 1:26.
24. *Zohar* 1:22b.
25. Gen 29:10–11.
26. *Zohar* 1:151b–152a.
27. Lev 23:11.
28. Lev 23.
29. Exod 19:1. See also Segal, "Shavuot, the Festival of Covenants"; Isaacs, "Shavuot History and Development."

wowed by the miracle of the Red Sea parting, feel her close presence. But, during the first stressful weeks in the wilderness, the Israelites lose heart. Their spiritual level falls; they lose touch with *Shechinah*.[30] Of course, she isn't far away; she is busy preparing to reconnect with her partner *tiferet*.[31] Seven weeks later, as the Israelites stand at Mt. Sinai, the two unite, overwhelming the people with their spiritual presence.

Sefirot in the Human Psyche

Kabbalists in the sixteenth century thought it important to stay in touch with the energy of the *sefirot*. They began to speak of their own spiritual potential in terms of the *sefirot*. A seeker might, for example, worry about their limited ability to love. But by drawing down the flow of divine *chesed*, they could correct their own weakness.[32] And—because the *sefirot* in the human soul are part of the single infinite divine continuum—each seeker's personal spiritual corrections *(tikkun)* could correct imbalances in divine energy itself.[33] So, each year between Passover and Shavuot, they re-enacted the inner drama of reconnecting with the *Shechinah*. They continued to call it a season of *Sefirat ha'Omer*, counting the ripening grain. But instead of counting grain, they took account of the *sefirot* moving inside them. They prepared to relive the revelation, not only of the Torah, but also of the *Shechinah*.[34]

Rabbi Isaac Luria, a sixteenth-century teacher of Kabbalah, designed a seven-week program for *Sefirat ha'Omer*. When we use his program—and it is popular right now—we focus on seven nuances within seven of the *sefirot*. We start with love and wind our way down to *Shechinah*. We take a week to observe each *sefirah*, noting each day how it interacts with one of the others.[35] Luria

---

30. *Zohar* 3:262a:10.

31. Giller, *Kabbalists of Beit El*, 87.

32. See, for example, Cordovero, *Palm Tree of Deborah*.

33. Scholem, *Major Trends in Jewish Mysticism*, Kindle.

34. Leader, "Sefirot Ha'Omer."

35. A sixteenth-century version of Luria's program is set out in Vital, *Pri*

taught his students to meditate on the *sefirot* as they mouthed familiar words of daily prayer.[36] I prefer to borrow an approach from the eighteenth-century Hasidic teacher, the Baal Shem Tov, discerning the *sefirot* present in my everyday experiences.[37] I also take inspiration from my fellow teachers of Jewish Renewal, a contemporary, socially progressive Kabbalistic movement.[38] We seek to re-integrate *Shechinah* into the divine in our own way, learning from teachers of every gender, and amplifying positive feminine faces of God.[39]

Feminine Faces of God

The Torah itself leaves room for diverse God-images. There's a lot of story and very little doctrine. Readers see God through the eyes of multiple characters. For example, Pharaoh sees in God a powerful king; Moses sees the essence of love; Hannah sees a compassionate manager of the world. So, it is really not surprising that Kabbalah explores multiple facets of divinity. In fact, the *Zohar* explicitly says that the divine appears to us differently in each generation.[40] To some biblical generations, it seems, the divine appeared as a mother. *Chochma*, Wisdom (or *Sophia*, in Greek), star of a fourth-century section of the book of Proverbs, describes herself as God's artisan.[41] *Ruach Elohim*, the spirit of God, hovers over the waters of creation like a mother bird.[42]

When an image keeps popping up in myths, images, and ideas, it is tempting to call it an "archetypal" image. Literally,

---

Etz Chaim, "Gate of the Omer Count, Chapter 2." For a contemporary version, see Jacobson, *Spiritual Guide to the Counting of the Omer.*

36. Giller, *Kabbalists of Beit El,* 44.

37. Green and Holtz, *Your Word Is Fire,* 101.

38. See, for example, Schachter-Shalomi, *Jewish with Feeling.*

39. See, for example, Novick, *On the Wings of Shechinah;* Gottlieb, *She Who Dwells Within;* Hammer, *Return to the Place;* Firestone, *The Receiving.*

40. *Zohar* 3:257b.

41. Prov 8:22–31; *Bereisheet Rabbah* 1:1.

42. Gen 1:2. See also, Duhan-Kaplan, *Mouth of the Donkey,* 56.

"archetype" means "ancient symbol." Depth psychologists have a theory about why these ancient symbols persist. Archetypes, they say, are part of the human psyche. Our species has a shared biological heritage, but we express it in culturally diverse ways.[43] Birthing, for example, is a universal part of our species' biology. But the social role of "mother" is culturally specific. Not that it's easy to pin down a culture's view of mothering—cultural traditions are complex and they are always in flux. North American culture, for example, constantly debates how much autonomy, economic support, and public voice mothers should have. And mothers themselves, particularly the most vulnerable among us, suffer. Practically speaking, our society needs to mend its relationship with mothers. Culturally speaking, it needs to heal its relationship with the archetypal mother, the *Shechinah*.

Sefirat Ha'Omer and Shechinah in This Book

Cultures change when many people learn together and act together.[44] Spiritual self-reflection is only one small part of the work. It is, however, the focus of this book. Here, I explore my own relationship with *Shechinah*, the archetypal mother. I find that I have great expectations. *Shechinah*, I believe, loves unconditionally, and she loves forever. Time and space do not matter to her; she loves you in life and in death. I love her too; I place my life in her hands. But I also find that no real person meets those expectations. My own disappointment—in my mother, my Aunt Sylvia, and myself—is huge. And, if I'm not careful, the disappointment can easily turn into anger, directed at all three of us. So, as I explore the seven *sefirot* of the *omer*, I look to find helpful ways to draw strength from my ideals.

The book continues with fifty short sections. Forty-nine explore nuances of the *sefirot*. The fiftieth explores the revelation at Mt. Sinai, aka the Ten Commandments. Throughout, I explore

43. Jacobi, *Complex, Archetype, Symbol.*

44. Bahá'í Community of Canada, "Advancing the Conversation on Reconciliation."

the *sefirot* as I see them reflected in everyday events. Most of these events take place right in our Sophia Street neighborhood, because that is where I wrote this book in spring of 2021, under COVID pandemic restrictions. They're small events, but they evoke big emotions like love, grief, and yearning. Because they bring to life spiritual, philosophical, and ethical questions, I write explicitly about those big ideas, too.

Writing has been part of my spiritual practice for almost fifty years. But it became even more important under pandemic restrictions. Our local spiritual leaders—who reached out to communities with tangible support—also encouraged us to find opportunities in our isolation. "Use this time for reflection," they said. "You have spiritual tools. Use them!"[45] So, I did, and this book is one result.

Join me on this spiritual journey of *Sefirat ha'Omer*. Read slowly, using the sections as daily *omer* prompts. Or read them all at once, following the stories and ideas as they layer and link in deepening cycles. Both are good ways to read. And both are good ways to move towards a renewed relationship with the *Shechinah*.

---

45. See, for example, *Distant Prayers* podcast.

Week One

Chesed

חסד

Love, Kindness

—— Day 1 ——

Chesed she'b'Chesed

Kindness within Love

L ove. Kindness. Both are good translations of the Hebrew word
chesed.

There are many different kinds of love. But today I want to
focus on family love. It's quite present to me in this COVID pandemic lockdown. My spouse and I and our young adult son are
together all the time. So we're working on our ability to love *all
the time*. Thus I am glad to reflect on today's quality: *chesed* within
chesed. Or, as I'll translate it, the kindness within love.

Some of that kindness comes easily. For example, it's our
habit to speak kind words. We say "please" and "thank you." Even
when someone simply does their household job. Why? Because
kindness holds our household system together. We work as a team
because we care. Because we want to make each other happy and
safe. So, we pay back kindness with kind words. "Thank you" can
mean "I appreciate your kindness."

But some of that kindness isn't so easy. Some habits are
harder to master. Patience, for example. Look, we all have different temperaments. We think and feel differently. But we're stuck
doing things together. So, sometimes a relative's behavior gets on
my nerves. Then I just want to shout, "Why do you always do it
this way?" "Can't you learn do this right?" "Do you have to be so
difficult?" But most of the time I don't shout at all. Because that
would not be kind. Instead, it would simply cause hurt. So, out

of kindness, I only scream in my mind. And there, I calm myself down, too. "Just let it go," I tell myself.

It's a load of inner work. But I—we—do it out of kindness. It's hard enough, we know, for a person to carry their own thoughts and feelings. So we don't want to drop an extra load on them. Instead, we hold our own feelings. We examine them, facet by facet. Just as this *omer* practice teaches!

——— Day 2 ———

Gevurah she'b'Chesed

Boundaries within Love

B oundaries. Strength. Good Judgment. You need these to love
well.

I'm always working on boundaries.

Sometimes, when someone I love asks me to do something,
I feel panic. Then, I pause before saying "yes." And I reflect.
What's the panic about? Do I not know how to do what's asked?
If so, can I learn quickly enough to be helpful? Or, do I know how
to do it, but don't have the time? If so, can I suggest a different
time frame? Or, a third possibility: Do I think what they're asking me to do is wrong? Unsafe to me or unkind to others? If so,
can I simply say "no"?

But to say "no" or even "yes, but later," I need good communication skills. Sure, there are some general strategies. Nonviolent
communication, for example, where I say what I'm feeling without blaming the other.[1] Compassionate listening, where I try to
empathize with the ask.[2] Constructive feedback techniques, where
I acknowledge what is good before I criticize.[3] Body language

---

1. Rosenberg, *Practical Spirituality*, 14–17.
2. Cohen, *Practicing the Art of Compassionate Listening*, Kindle.
3. Brounstein, *Coaching and Mentoring*, 71.

awareness, where I stay relaxed.[4] But really there are no good one-size-fits-all strategies. It's always a judgment call.

So, yes, good boundaries depend on self-awareness. And also on other-awareness. And on empathy, an ability to see from a loved one's point of view, and to sometimes see yourself and your own behavior from their point of view. But how much other-awareness is too much?

One year, I put a mini disco ball on our Passover Seder plate. I told my guests it represents multiple perspectives, the kind we welcome in Seder discussion. And it did spark some good discussion. But last night, the disco ball came back to me in a dream. More of a nightmare, really. The disco ball spun inside my head, each mirror showing a view of me through someone else's eyes. And I woke in a panic.

Each person, I thought, acts as though their view of me is true. And, if I'm not really what they see, they get upset. With me. And sometimes that makes me anxious. But do I have to please them? How much pleasing is too much? Or too little? How sensitive should I be?

4. Guenther, *Holy Listening*, 33–37.

——— Day 3 ———

Tiferet she'b'Chesed

Beauty within Love

I want the people I love to find me beautiful. What do I hope they'll see? I hope my children will see me as wise, calm, and kind. And I hope my spouse will see me as . . . actually, I'm not sure. Something good?

Maybe the details don't matter. I'm just hoping for his unconditional positive regard. I want him to accept me and support me no matter what. Maybe I've been crabby or inattentive. Or mismanaged money, ignored an in-law, left him a mess to clean up. By all means, he can let me know I was wrong, even that I hurt him. But, even then, I want his unconditional positive regard[1] to shine through.

But is this fair?

Ideally, a parent will show a child unconditional love. Psychologically, this helps a child grow up safely. They can make mistakes, and learn from them. And not worry that each mistake is a total fail. My late mother showed me this love. In a real-life way, of course, mixed with plenty of confusion, yelling, and punishing. But, tough as it was, it was unconditional love. Nothing I did could shake it. She loved me because I exist. To her, I was beautiful, even on our bad days.

---

1. Rogers, *On Becoming a Person,* 34.

Mom is gone now. And I look to my spouse to take her place. But his mother is gone, too. Probably, he looks to me to take *her* place. To shine a little unconditional positive regard his way. And to remind him how beautiful he is. But do either of us have the energy to do this? When we're both drained of our own unconditional love sources?

─── Day 4 ───

Netzach she'b'Chesed

Eternity within Love

F orever Love.
   What does that even look like? Like a mother's love? Maybe?

We talked about that today, in the online Sacred Texts and Oral Traditions class that I teach. So many cultures tell stories about the Mother of all life. Why, we asked, is this archetype so powerful?

Because, I said, we believe in an ideal mother. But none of us gets one. We only get a real mother.

Students then spoke of their mothers. "I was adopted and when I found my birth mother, she rejected me." "My mother was hard on me, but we worked it out." "Now I understand my mother was very young, so I forgive her."

In their minds, the students knew: we only get a real mother. But in their hearts, they yearned for something else. A mother who would love them before they were born, while they were alive, and after they died. A perfect love, forever.

Each morning, they woke up hoping. And each day they cried themselves to sleep, disappointed. Maybe not literally. But that's how deeply their hearts were broken.

The prophet Isaiah understands. Channeling God, he says: *Can a woman forget her baby, Or disown the child of her womb? Though she might forget, I never could forget you.*[1]

The ideal mother, Isaiah says, loves her child, forever. But maybe the only mother you saw up close wasn't ideal. Maybe she was only real. And maybe she did forget you, sometimes. But don't despair, he says. You do have an ideal mother. A forever being, not bound by time or space, who loves you forever.

Maybe the cultural stories about first Mothers say something like that, too. We all have a mythical mother, alive beyond time and space. She's always there for us to turn to.

Maybe she is like the Potawatomi Sky Woman,[2] who shares the love she got from the animals. Or the Torah's Eve, who loves despite the pain it brings her.[3] Or the Qur'an's Mrs. Adam,[4] steady supervisor of the world household. Or Mary Magdalene of John's Gospel, a caring spiritual teacher.[5]

She doesn't live on earth. But maybe she lives in our hearts.

---

1. Isa 49:15.

2. Kimmerer, *Braiding Sweetgrass*, 2–4.

3. Gen 2–4.

4. Qur'an 2:30–39; See also Mir, *Understanding the Islamic Scripture*, Kindle.

5. John 20:14–17.

—— Day 5 ——

Hod she'b'Chesed

Gratitude within Love

B enedictine spiritual teachers say: gratitude grounds our relationship with God.[1] What do they mean?

Sit down when you're in a funk, make a list of things you're grateful for, and you'll see. Gratitude lifts us out of constricted consciousness. It connects us with something greater.

So, here's an analogy. A loose one, but maybe a helpful one.

Appreciation grounds our human relationships. When we turn our attention to what others do right, not what they do wrong, friendship is easier.

I have worked on my appreciation skills for many years. One technique I use is careful speech. I try to speak in a positive way. *Not:* Your writing is all over the place. *But:* You're interested in so many things! *Not:* You left the dishes for me again! *But:* I see how absorbed you are in your work.

Words are more tangible than thoughts or feelings. For years, I worked on changing my habits of speech.[2] Then, because I had to think more carefully before I spoke, my habits of thought changed. So, the way I understood my emotions changed. And then, my feelings changed too.

1. Hamm, "Rummaging for God."
2. One helpful tool was Finkelman and Berkowitz, *Chofetz Chaim.*

So it's easier, now, to be grounded in that happy place. Here, I am less easily upset. Less irritated, less angry. More appreciative, more loving.

But this approach is not for everyone. In fact, I've been criticized for it.

A congregant once said, "I wish were you more like a righteously angry Moses and less like a peacemaking Aaron."

A colleague regularly rolls his eyes and says, "You are far more generous than I am."

A friend often says, "You give people the benefit of the doubt too often."

Even my daughter sometimes says, "Stop it, Mom!"

Sigh. When do I get to reflect on the humor in love? On how much fun difference can be?

Day 6

Yesod she'b'Chesed

Foundation within Love

What is the foundation of love?

Sometimes, it's a freely given act of love or care. Like caring for those who have died. Because you don't expect them to give you anything in return.

A story, a real one from five years ago, comes to mind.

"Mom, mom, mom, mom," says my young adult son. "Not-Koi is in front of our house and he's not moving."

Not-Koi is a neighbor, a yellow tabby cat, a long-time friend of our yellow tabby Koi. The two cats look so much alike, that we simply call them Koi and Not-Koi.

"He's really elderly," I say. "He's really deaf. You can walk right by him and he won't move."

"Mom, I think this is different. He's, like, *really* not moving."

I come outside to see Not-Koi lying peacefully on his side, eyes open. He is not moving at all, not even breathing.

He's wearing his signature light fabric collar. Gently I remove it, hoping to find a phone number. There it is, barely legible, in fading permanent marker, next to the word "Auto."

The number rings ten times. No answer. I phone again. Straight to voice mail. I phone again. This time, a sleepy voice answers. "Hello?"

"Are you the owner of an elderly yellow tabby?" I ask.

"Yellow taxi?" He sounds confused.

"Tabby. Cat."

"Yes."

"He appears to have passed away peacefully in our yard."

"I'll be over in about an hour."

Leave a corpse lying for an hour in the hot summer sun? No.

"I'm going to wrap him in a towel and bring him inside. There are lots of bugs out here."

"What is your address? Will someone be home?"

"Sophia Street. Yes, we'll be home."

Not-Koi's rigid body and heavy weight surprise me. I wrap him in a white towel; lay him in white laundry basket; place his collar carefully on top.

A text message arrives: I'm heading over now. Be there in 5 minutes or less—Marc.

A young man stands at the door, cat carrier in hand. "I'm Marc."

"I'm Laura. I'm so sorry. His name is Auto?"

"Yes."

"He's been coming to our yard for about two years. He's friends with our cats."

"Yeah, he got sick about a year ago."

"Thyroid condition?" I'd noticed his weight loss; fed his hunger.

"Yes."

"He's not been hearing so well, either."

"We noticed that," Marc says.

He reaches for the tiny cat carrier, but I stop him. "It's pretty recent, so he's still stiff. Take our laundry basket. It's just from the dollar store."

"We just live over on Walden," he replies.

We want to make conversation, but no words come. Marc takes Auto and goes.

Two hours later, I text a year-old photo of Auto (aka Not-Koi) and Koi.

—Marc, thought you might appreciate this photo of feline friends relaxing together—Laura & family

—Aww. Thanks for that. Sometimes when we saw your cat over here we would call for Auto and realize: oh, that's "Auto-alike."

—We called Auto "Not-Koi."

—Haha!

Two hours later, Marc texts again.

—A token of thanks on your front steps

It's a huge bouquet of marigolds with a note: *Thank you for befriending Auto over the last few years of his life. Thank you for taking such good care of him at his passing.—M. and N.*[1]

1. Duhan-Kaplan, "Death of a Cat," *Sophia Street*.

Day 7

Shechinah she'b'Chesed

Presence within Love

When I was a newlywed, I thought a lot about presence in love-making. How to be fully present to your own experience. And also be fully present as part of a team of two. How to be open to your own joy. And also to a shared joy. To an experience in your body. And also to an experience that transcends your body.

A few things I learned in yoga helped. Breathe together. Look with a soft gaze and a smile. Imagine you're sending love from one heart to another.

Now, years later, I know these are great tools of empathy. I use them when I'm teaching or offering spiritual direction. But I wish I used them more often. I wish I remembered them more often. Yes, I wish I was present with full awareness more often.

Sometimes I imagine this presence is a bit like the Force, in Star Wars. You can use it to change the way people feel. But it's a force that should only be used for good, to uplift people.

Being present in these ways always uplifts me. It changes my consciousness. Somehow, it's easier to access wonder. I'm not sure why; I haven't quite articulated it to myself. Maybe it turns my attention outwards? So that there's less mental chatter, blocking things? Or so that I don't just see my own projections everywhere I look?

Here's something else I'm not sure of. Why do I so easily forget to be present? It's not hard work. And it feels great. But maybe sometimes I just get tired? I feel forlorn, and wish that the ideal mother would hold me. That *Shechinah* would hold me in her presence, hold me in her love.

Week Two

Gevurah

גבורה

Judgment, Boundaries,
Justice

—— Day 8 ——

Chesed she'b'Gevurah

Love within Judgment

Judgment tempered by Love.

My husband Charles is a cognitive psychologist. So he has thought a lot about how minds work. How people collect information, organize it, and use it to make judgments. So, today I interviewed him.

Here's a bit of what he said.

Raw judgment is dangerous. Let me explain what I mean. "Judgment" is finding fault in people. "Raw" means it's not tempered by the other sefirot. "Dangerous" means it pushes you down a rabbit hole. Where the person you're judging becomes more and more of a negative figure.

Then, we started talking about case studies. Suppose you are parent to a young adult child. They're not in danger. But you don't think they are making good decisions. So, you worry about them all the time. Should you say so? How often? How strongly?

Suppose they already know what you think. And they look at you with a searching expression. As if they're asking, "Are you judging me? Right now?" And suppose it breaks your heart. What can you do?

Here's what my husband said next.

You can keep the struggle internal. You don't have to stop the thoughts. But try not to express them. It's okay to notice that you want a person to be different. But remember that you love them. And when you love someone, you don't focus on their faults.

Really, all people are flawed. Falling in love isn't about finding a perfect person. Instead, it's about finding someone whose quirks you're willing to live with. And that's a commitment.

My husband's approach isn't the same as mine. I want to burn away all negative judgments with a spiritual fire. But he accepts their existence, and looks for strategies to counter them.

—— Day 9 ——

Gevurah she'b'Gevurah

Judgment within Judgment

I 've been waiting for this one. Why? Well, my memory might be a little fuzzy. But I'm pretty sure I wrote my philosophy PhD dissertation about this.[1]

So much, I wrote, goes into making good judgments. You have to listen and read carefully. Understand a social and political environment. See how power works and thus learn to problem-solve well. Observe the effects of your decisions and evaluate your ethics. You must draw good logical inferences. But also know when to set logic aside for imagination. Use metaphors to make new connections. But also recognize when you see only your projections instead of what's real.

Whoa. When I put it that way, making good judgments seems like a lot of work. Every judgment is an avalanche of mini-judgments. Is avalanche the right word? Maybe it's more like a maze. Or an obstacle course.

Sometimes, when I'm agonizing over something, it does feel that way. But, more often, all the details come together in a single intuition. If you ask me to explain, I might talk about politics, power, or ethics. About logic, imagination, or separating myself from a situation. Because it all factors in, somehow.

1. Duhan-Kaplan, "The Critical Thinking Movement" (PhD, 1991).

Somehow. And here's where I second-guess myself. Am I actually wise? Or do I make that other stuff up as an afterthought, a justification? Can I tell when my explanation is genuine? Or when, instead, I'm lying to myself a little bit?

Good judgment, I think, should start with an uncompromising search for truth. And then use that truth in a nuanced way. Maybe to craft a compromise. But, if I can't trust my truth, will my compromise be a good one?

Here's a simple example. When I teach in my inter-religious classroom, I try to be aware of students' inter-generational trauma.[2] Using my family and cultural history, I try to understand and empathize. And then I try to teach in a nuanced way. But what if read my students' cues poorly? Misunderstand the political context? Don't really see how power works in the classroom? And what if I can't tell when I'm wrong?

---

2. Duhan-Kaplan, "Healing Social Trauma."

—— Day 10 ——

Tiferet she'b'Gevurah

Beauty within Judgment

At its best, judgment activates our rational minds. So, let's take a theory break. A little detour into philosophy.

Plato's allegory of the cave tells of prisoners chained to a bench. Where they sit, they can only see shadows. So they think and talk only about shadows. One day, though, a prisoner escapes and climbs out of the cave. Outside, she sees the sun and the objects that cast shadows. Now, she understands the shadows for what they were. And she has a new sense of what is real.[1]

It's a metaphor, of course. For the difference between ordinary consciousness and spiritual perception. In everyday life, we're easily distracted by shadows: rumor, gossip, propaganda, advertising, material comfort. But when we step out of this habit, we see what really matters. The highest values: justice, beauty, goodness, truth, equality.

Over time, we learn to judge ourselves by these values. We hope, for example, for justice. So, in our communities, we design policies and fair procedures. But then a case study shows they don't always lead to justice. So, guided by the value of justice, we try to do better.

Plato's ideas are reflected in the *sefirot*. They, too, are big values that guide our lives. As per philosophers and Kabbalists, *sefirot*

---

1. Plato, *Republic* 514a–520a.

are the building blocks of human nature. So of course we judge ourselves by them! We evaluate our real lives using these ideals. Is our love loving enough? Our judgment discerning enough?

Each *sefirah*, in a way, sets a standard of spiritual beauty. That's refreshing. But it's also challenging. Because I'm used to thinking that beauty standards are unattainable. So, the instant I feel I've met a goal, I also feel I've missed it.

Today, at work, I received a written personnel evaluation. (Spoiler alert: it was fine.) The author is not a Kabbalist. Still, they talked about every single one of the *sefirot*. Love, judgment, compassion, endurance, gratitude, foundation, and presence.

Reading it, I was unsettled. All my evaluators have seen, I thought, are shadows on the cave wall. It's true, I *try* to live by the ideals they listed. But I know how far I fall short. So, I am not sure what they see.

So, here's a question. A self-question, that is. Self-evaluation is great. But as a relentless habit it can be painful. So, how do I find a beautiful balance between seeking the ideal and appreciating the real?

——— Day 11 ———

Netzach she'b'Gevurah

Endurance within Judgment

E ver read evaluations of your own teaching? Or an event you led?

If so, then you know. You might get twenty-eight positive comments, with one negative outlier. And what do you remember best? What lingers longest in your thoughts and hurts your heart the most? The one negative comment, of course. Even if it comes from a mere acquaintance. Or even a stranger.

But some people are more important than mere strangers. Early caregivers, for example. You watch them carefully for cues about how to be in this world. You respond to those cues. And your responses become your habits of thought, feeling, and action.

What happens when they judge you negatively? I don't mean once, out of grief, anger, or fear. But regularly, habitually. How does that form you?

I was raised by my mother and my father and my Aunt Sylvia. My father always tried to build up my confidence. But Mom and Aunt Sylvia weren't that careful. If they thought I mis-stepped, they let me know. Lovingly, but sometimes sarcastically. Especially when I became a young adult. At least, that's how I remember it.

I didn't call or write home very often. Probably I was full-up with work and school. And I needed all the alone time I could get just to be quiet.

When I did call, Aunt Sylvia would say, "Well, how do you do!!!"

Mom was more direct, "You never call your mother!"

This went on for thirty-five years.

So I came to think of myself as someone who falls out of touch. Someone who should be ashamed of herself. And who, when she does reach out, will be received with sarcasm and scolding.

Well, you know how that goes. When I miss a friend, I immediately feel ashamed. When I think of reaching out, I picture them scolding me. So what do I do? I put it off again.

But here's the thing. No one, except Mom and Aunt Sylvia, has ever scolded me for reaching out. And even Mom changed in the last few years of her life. When I'd call, she would say, "Hello, I love you."

But the negative judgments endure. And, I am still afraid to reach out if weeks or months have passed.

This morning, a friend died of COVID. Almost a year to the day since we last talked by phone. Over the year, I thought of her often. The more I missed her, the more ashamed I felt. So, I put off the call.

Today I just feel sad. And I see, so clearly, how some old judgments get in my way. Especially the judgments planted in a much younger me, by people who finished raising me a long time ago.

—— Day 12 ——

Hod she'b'Gevurah

Splendor within Judgment

I don't teach philosophy anymore, and I'm glad. But I learned so much from it.

Philosophy is equal parts critical thinking and creative thinking. In the critical thinking part, you have to define concepts precisely. Think quickly about all the implications of each definition. Follow each line of thinking with immaculate logic. Choose the best conclusion. And then explain what's wrong with it.

In the creative part, you get to pick a topic people normally don't pay attention to. Something that hides in the fabric of everyday life. You notice it, wonder about it, ask startling questions. And, as soon as an answer seems familiar, you let it go. Then you push your mind in a new direction. Towards the edges of what you used to think about. And then beyond.

But (ideally) you never become unhinged. Because logic grounds you.

Not everyone appreciates philosophers.[1] Some people think that we are rigidly intellectual. Think that we need to loosen our grip on thinking once in a while, and turn, instead, towards something more spiritual. But they don't realize: pushing at the boundaries of our concepts is a *spiritual* experience. It's our way of seeking deeper truths.

1. Plato, *Phaedo* 64b.

Of course, not all philosophers are interested in self-reflection, in soul-accounting, or *cheshbon hanefesh,* as we call it in Hebrew.[2] But some of us are. And, maybe now, I should speak in the first person. *I am very into cheshbon hanefesh.* And I use the habits of thought I learned in philosophy.

For example, I might notice a movement of thought or feeling that doesn't feel right. Then I'll try to define carefully what it is. I'll ask myself questions about it. Find some tentative answers. Notice they're not quite right. Ask a few more questions.

And, as I go through the steps, my thought and feeling begin to change. Because I'm pushing at the edges of what I used to think. And maybe going beyond them.

2. Alan Morinis, *Everyday Holiness,* 261.

—— Day 13 ——

Yesod she'b'Gevurah

Foundation within Judgment

What are the foundations of judgment? Are they feelings? Beliefs? Can we free ourselves from old foundations? See the world anew? And then learn to make kinder, gentler judgments?

Apparently, academics are debating this right now.

Some "affect theorists" believe we will never know the foundations of our judgment. How could we? We humans don't experience raw affect. Instead, social context, recent thoughts, future hopes all shape our feeling. Feelings come into our bodies already interpreted.[1]

But other affect theorists disagree. Sensation exists for a split second before we interpret it. So does emotion. And I think I am on this team.

Recently, I had a great conversation about this with a colleague. He is a spiritual teacher in a Hindu tradition.[2] One mentor taught him a powerful mantra. "If you chant these words," the mentor said, "you will never again erupt in anger."

So, we talked about what it means to "chant a mantra." We identified four levels of "chanting."

First level: Chant it out loud. Learn it. Sing it out. Memorize it. Feel its rhythm in your body.

1. Seigworth and Gregg, "An Inventory of Shimmers."
2. Pandit Tejomaya, personal communication.

Second level: Chant it in a whisper. Watch your behavior. If you find yourself expressing anger, remember the mantra. Whisper the words and calm yourself.

Third level: Chant it in your thoughts. Observe them. For example, when you feel irritated, where do your thoughts go? Do you leap to blame others? If so, think of the mantra. Use it as a counter-thought.

Fourth level: Chant it in your feelings. Chant it before your anger even arises. But you can't make this one happen. It comes after you've used the mantra well. Eventually, the mantra chants itself.

Can the mantra really chant itself? I think it can.

In fact, I have a personal example.

Some days, I am overwhelmed with professional jealousy. In the age of social media, everyone looks so successful. Everyone has impressive posts and bios. Everyone except me, that is. Here I am, four decades into my career. I've worked so hard! How can others outrun me just using fancy pics and videos? My jealous feelings don't help me. They just diminish me in my own eyes. They leave me sad and anxious, run down and hopeless.

So, I adopted an anti-jealousy mantra. It's not an original mantra; I learned it from Buddhist teachers. *May you be happy.*[3]

I practiced at the first level, repeating it a few minutes a day.

Then, I took it to the second level, whispering it when I felt jealous.

At the third level, it began to pop up automatically, whenever I felt jealous as a kind of counter-thought. As if my mind itself said, "Don't think that! Think this instead!"

And now at the fourth level—not always, but often—I hear of a colleague's success and I feel happy. And my first thought is: how nice for them!

Honestly, it didn't come easily or quickly. But somehow, I slipped under the foundation of my judgment. And I built a new foundation.

---

3. Bernhard, *How to Be Sick*, 45–56.

———— Day 14 ————

Shechinah she'b'Gevurah

Cosmic Mother within Judgment

Today I just want to celebrate the wisdom of the Great Mother. Or, as she's known in ordinary English, a grandmother.

Last night I dreamed:

I am driving on a five-lane highway. Everyone is going in the same direction. So, the road is very crowded. "Maybe I should turn back," I think. But I don't.

Then I realize the road becomes a bridge over big water. "Maybe I should turn back now," I think, "because, the next chance is far away." But I don't.

Then the bridge ends abruptly. So I shut off my car and get out. I walk to the side of the road, to one of the bridge's towers. A door leads into the tower. Two grey-haired women walk in. They are going downstairs, where they will walk an underground path. It will take them to a place they can turn their cars in the right direction.

I follow them.

Do I even need to interpret this? The message seems obvious. Everyone's going in the wrong direction. They're ignoring all the warnings. Finally, their only choice is to stop. And then follow the grandmothers' deep wisdom so we can turn ourselves around.

The biblical book of Proverbs *(Mishlei)* says, "Do not forsake the teachings of your mother."[1]

---

1. Prov 1:8, translation mine.

What does Proverbs think mothers teach? First, cosmic wisdom: how the world works, and how to play in it.[2] And second, practical wisdom. Mothers seem to know how to do everything. Sew, shop, buy real estate, support the needy. Speak wisely, kindly, cheerfully. And dress like a queen, too.[3]

Of course I can critique this; clearly it's hyperbole. But, for the moment, let's assume it's true.

How do we learn all this practical wisdom? Through experience. And the older we are, the more experience we have. We watch, absorb, try, evaluate, adapt. It's a cycle of learning. The more we do it, the better we get. So, the older we are, the wiser we are.

I'm still a very young elder. But I already have lots of cosmic wisdom. And I have practical skills, too. I can free fingers stuck together with gorilla glue, remove an unruly person from a room, and cook a great meal with whatever's in the pantry. And, like the grandmothers in my dream, I also have some deep wisdom. I'm getting better at finding my direction and turning myself around.

Truth? That last one is a new skill. Because nine years ago, I lost my direction. In fact, when my own mother died, I thought my life was over. If I've raised my children and buried my parents, I asked, what life tasks are left? But I pressed on, without joy at first. And then I found the inner mother. She taught me, all over again, how to play in the world.

2. Prov 8.
3. Prov 31.

Week Three

Tiferet

תפארת

Beauty, Balance

—— Day 15 ——

Chesed she'b'Tiferet

Love within Beauty

L ove that sees beauty. And love that seeks beauty.

"Beauty is in the eye of the beholder." At the simplest level, this means we all find different things beautiful. When we love someone, for example, they seem beautiful to us. Like my cat Koi. He's an ordinary-looking orange tabby. And, at age sixteen, he's got some scars. But, to me, he is still the most beautiful cat in the world.

But the phrase has deeper meanings too. It focuses on "the eye of the beholder." On the inner experience of beauty: the sudden sense of peace that rushes in, makes you certain that this little part of the world is perfect, and that maybe the whole world could be perfect too. Then, you yearn for perfection, even as you're surrounded by it. It sounds self-contradictory, but it feels just right.

This sounds a lot like the experience of love. At least, that's how Plato describes it in his book *Symposium*. Love, he says is a longing to see beauty forever.[1]

I'm a parent of young adult children. And I love them deeply. So I find them very beautiful. I want to see them forever—literally. Thus, I would love for them to stay close. But I also want them to find their own beauty. Their own partners, passions, paths. For that, they need some distance.

1. Plato, *Symposium,* 204d–209e.

Really, I want them to be close and far at the same time. This also sounds self-contradictory. But, really, it's not. It's just a delicate juggling act. I want them to know how precious they are to me. And also how fully I trust them. (Even when I don't.)

So, often, I ask myself these questions. In their times of distress, am I available enough? Supportive, but without solving their problems for them? In their times of joy, am I interested enough? Asking them just the right questions, but not too often?

I hope my children find our family love beautiful. I want them to feel that this little corner of the universe is safe. And, thus, that the rest of the universe could be safe too.

Day 16

Gevurah she'b'Tiferet

Justice within Beauty

How does beauty hold justice in it?

Well, there's Plato's view, that all ideals converge. The best things are good, beautiful, and just. So when we see something truly beautiful, it's because we also see justice in action. Injustice is ugly, and we find it jarring.

And there's Simone Weil's view. Humans never stop hoping for beauty. So, we expect the good, no matter what terrible things happen to us. We expect justice. And thus injustice, when it happens, is a shock.[1]

Both these philosophers say: beauty points us towards justice.

But that's not my experience. Instead, many people turn away when they see injustice. They seek shelter in beauty. If they can, that is. In a beautiful life, neighborhood, family—where questions of justice and injustice don't even come up. And where ugliness doesn't disrupt them.

Our yearning for beauty pulls us in two directions. Into action. And into quietude.

Sometimes, injustice is a matter of your own life and death. And then you show up. You assemble, write, speak, paint, teach, feed, support. Whatever you can learn how to do. And whatever creates a beautiful community of resistance.

---

1. Presler, "Weil on Power," 133–34.

But sometimes injustice is a matter of someone else's life and death. And then it's tempting to retreat into a cloistered kind of beauty. *Even when your conscience screams that it's wrong.*

—— Day 17 ——

Tiferet she'b'Tiferet

Beauty within Beauty

The heart of the tree of *sefirot*.

Some say the vibe of *tiferet* is like the vibe of *YHWH*: the ineffable divine, subtle like a breath. But also, like a breath, threading through everything we do.[1]

Occasionally beauty catches our attention. It leaps forward and touches our psyche. And it leaves a permanent trace: an image, loaded with feeling. It's a "poetic moment," says philosopher Gaston Bachelard. We can analyze it, of course. But that comes later. In the moment, we are too full.[2]

Poetic moments can be gentle and inviting. Sublime and sweet. But they can also be terrifying. More like what theologian Rudolph Otto calls a "numinous" experience. An "eruption" of the holy into our world.[3]

Numinous experiences come in dreams, too. Here's one I had recently:

I am on a mountaintop, in a large cabin. Dozens of people sit on the floor. Older Habonim-Dror [youth movement] members are leading a seminar. It's interesting, congenial, I enjoy it. But I leave the cabin anyway. I walk along a rocky trail on the mountainside.

1. Waskow, *God's Earthquake*, 12.
2. Bachelard, *Poetics of Space*, xi–xiv.
3. Otto, *Idea of the Holy*, 5–7, 196.

Other people walk it, too. But we are far apart, each walking alone. Suddenly, we all stop and turn in awe. Hovering near us is a giant condor. It faces us, brown wings outstretched, showing us its bright blue belly. On its head are three little upright feathers, like quail feathers, only blue.

Sure, I could analyze it. I'm on a mountaintop, a peak, close to heaven. But I'm in an enclosed space, receiving religious teachings. It's an open-minded tradition and I enjoy it. But I step outside of it to walk a rockier path. Others walk solitary paths there too. And that's where we see beauty. A terrifying beauty. A numinous beauty, showing itself to us. A hybrid beauty, a new synthesis, part condor, part peacock. And all we can do is gawk.

But the analysis pales next to the dream's power. Next to the bird's beauty. Yes, the analysis says, "Go outside the box." It's a good message. But it puts the dream in a box. Yes, it seems to follow the dream's metaphor. But too quickly, too neatly.

So, when I woke up, I didn't analyze the dream. Instead, I googled "peacock condor." And I found some amazing images of peacocks in flight. Now, when I look at them, the feeling of the dream comes back. The poetic moment lives in me again.

Maybe the dream has no message other than, "Pay attention."

Day 18

Netzach she'b'Tiferet

Eternity within Beauty

L asting beauty.

I want beautiful things to last forever. But isn't that a kind of attachment? One best met with non-attachment practice?

But where do I begin? Maybe with last night's dream.

We discover harmful bacteria in our pond. Then, I notice blue ink stains all over my white dress. And bits of paper stuck to my face. I pull them off, leaving my face swollen and bruised. One friend says another stopped using her husband's last name. Suddenly, I'm travelling on a train with no windows. When I get out, I'm in Charlotte, North Carolina.

This dream takes me on a tour of little luxuries I take for granted. Safe drinking water. Clean clothes. Healthcare. Intact family. A familiar place to live. And then the dream takes each one away.

So, it makes me ask myself, "What if you lost these, Laura? Could you adapt, as so many have had to? How attached are you?"

But the dream also shows my existential attachments. I want to write without being stained by controversy. Show a good face to the world. Know where I'm going in life.

So, I ask myself, "Could you give up any of *these* attachments, Laura? What if you weren't so cautious? So concerned about reputation? So risk-averse? Could you do more to help others?"

At some point, these attachments helped steer me in a good direction. But the world changes. My life changes. So my standards of social and moral beauty could change, too.

—— Day 19 ——

Hod she'b'Tiferet

Gratitude within Beauty

I t's spring in the rain forest. So, I get to see lots of beautiful things. Cherry blossoms. Bees in flowers. Robins grazing in early gardens.

In this season, I often feel overwhelmed by beauty. So, sometimes, I can't believe my good fortune. How did I manage to be here in this exact moment of blossoming, foraging, grazing? This moment of grace?

I also feel overwhelmed with gratitude. And want to say "Thank you!" But I don't know who to thank. The creatures? But they just happen to be here too. The Creator? That's a soaring thought. The ineffable magic that links us all?

One famous Hebrew blessing holds it all: *Bless you God, Ineffable yet revealed in Creation and Present in all realities—**just because it's like this in your world.**[1]*

Now that is an attitude of "radical amazement." That's Abraham Joshua Heschel's name for spiritual perception. It's a way of seeing the world, where everything points beyond itself.[2] To God, of course. But not to God the super person, force, or cause. Instead: to what is ineffable, revealed in creation, present in all realities.

---

1. Translation inspired by Prager, *Path of Blessing.*
2. Heschel, *God in Search of Man,* 45–47.

If you see with radical amazement, then *it's always like this in the world*. It's not always pretty. But it is always beautiful, always overwhelming. Because you see and you feel. Even when you don't know why or how. Or even whom to ask.

So, how am I doing with spiritual perception? Do I see with radical amazement all the time? No, obviously not. Much of the time I'm just in a funk.

Sometimes a flower, a bee, or a bird lifts me up. But when they're not around . . . ? Where do I find my fix of beauty?

—— Day 20 ——

Yesod she'b'Tiferet

Foundation within Beauty

W hat's the foundation of a beautiful soul?
Repetition. Not the kind that goes in circles. But in cycles.

Teachers know. When we want to lay a foundation for a good habit, we use repetition. We say things over and over again. And we ask the learners to do them over and over again.

So, today I realized something. *Sefirat ha'Omer* can be really repetitive! The beauty in love. Then the love in beauty. Then the love in splendor. And the splendor in love.

So I wondered. How many places can I really go with this journey? Where else can the concepts shine a light? Haven't they already revealed so much? Why is there so much repetition?

And then, of course, I saw something new. *Sefirat ha'Omer* is supposed to be repetitive. That's the whole point. You go back and keep shining the light in the same places. And then you see new things.

So, I'd like to come back to my dream of two days ago. And then ask: what does it say about the foundation of a soul?

We discover harmful bacteria in our pond. Then, I notice blue ink stains all over my white dress. And bits of paper stuck to my face. I pull them off, leaving my face swollen and bruised. One friend says another stopped using her husband's last name.

Suddenly, I'm travelling on a train with no windows. When I get out, I'm in Charlotte, North Carolina.

So, symbol by symbol:

The pond. Water often represents the unconscious.[1] This water isn't overwhelming, like the ocean is. And yes, bacteria—negative stuff—swim around. But they are dangerous only if you drink them in. It's still safe to visit the pond.

The white dress. Specifically, it's the one I wear on Yom Kippur. So, it hints at the pure soul I hope to be at the end of the ritual. But this pure soul is stained with the ink of my writing. With what leaks out as I prepare neat blog posts for public consumption.

My face, covered. But partly revealed, and partly bruised. Is this the face I show others? Or the face I show myself? All I know for sure: when I peel off the paper, I see a face in need of healing.

Name change. Identity. It's mine alone. I am me. Not other family members. And not the audience I imagine I write for.

Travels. To a place I used to live. I'm going back again, to see what more there is to learn.

So, as *Sefirat ha'Omer* brings me around again to similar prompts, I ask: How can I go deeper? What can I draw up from the unconscious? Can I take up things that leaked in a previous reflection? What do I see that is for my eyes, my heart, alone?

Maybe I'll need all forty-nine days to answer these questions. I'm not sure why I should be surprised. I mean, you don't say, "I've mastered spiritual practice." "I have achieved enlightenment." "I don't need Yom Kippur ever again." "I did psychotherapy when I was twenty-one, so I dealt with everything." Instead, you ride the train over and over again, and then see where it takes you.

---

1. Collinson, "Water."

Day 21

Shechinah she'b'Tiferet

Presence within Beauty

I'd like to talk about Presence. But with a few conceptual details along the way. And a little story about the biblical character Rachel.

Sefirot, we know, are spiritual qualities. Shapes and styles of divine expression. And of human psychology.

If the *sefirot* underlie everything, then where are they in the Torah? *Everywhere*, says the *Zohar*, the big book of Jewish mysticism. Because the entire Torah is an allegory for the life of the *sefirot*.

But, to see *sefirot* in the Torah, you need a few tools. A few hints that will help you crack the code. It's helpful to know, for example, which characters represent which *sefirot*.

Stories about Jacob teach us about *tiferet*, beauty or balance. Why? His grandfather, Abraham, receives *chesed*, love and kindness. And his father, Isaac, traumatized as a youth, receives *gevurah*, judgment. So, Jacob has a bit of each in him. He has to find his own path of *tiferet*, balance and beauty.

And stories about Rachel teach us about *malchut*, royalty, also known as *Shechinah*, maternal presence of God. Why? Because she is the mother of the Jewish people—so says the prophet

Jeremiah.[1] And because her wise words can turn God's heart towards compassion.[2]

The Torah tells us that there is a bit of Rachel inside of Jacob. Or, rather, that Jacob is touched by Rachel's wisdom. And, somehow, he absorbs it.

As a young co-wife, Rachel is at odds with her sister. But, eventually, she lets go of the conflict. She says, "I have wrestled with my sister, with holy wrestling, and I have won."[3]

A few years pass.

Jacob is estranged from his brother. But his brother seeks him out. And just before they meet, Jacob wrestles with a mysterious stranger. Then the stranger says, "You have wrestled with God and humans, and you have won."[4]

The Torah is quite clear, in its understated way. Rachel does her inner work, and makes peace with her sibling. Her husband Jacob watches her. And, as best he can, he tries to do what she does. He absorbs her wisdom. Thus, he heals a rift inside his own heart.[5]

Here, it's easy to think of Rachel as *Shechinah*. A kind of divine mother. She has wisdom, and she is a role model. Does she know she's Jacob's teacher, or is she just living her best life?

It's a heavy responsibility, to know you're a teacher and a role model. And that others treat you as one. Especially when you're barely holding it together yourself. Then, you're sure they're seeing a projection, some mother archetype, but they're not seeing the real you. Still, you don't want to fail them. You want to be the wise presence they need. Did I say "you"? I mean "me."

---

1. Jer 31:14–16.

2. *Lamentations Rabbah* 24.

3. Gen 30:8.

4. Gen 32:29.

5. Pardes, *Countertraditions,* 60–78.

Week Four

Netzach

נצח

Endurance, Eternity

Day 22

Chesed she'b'Netzach

Love within Endurance

L ove that keeps us keeping on.

Today, I'd like to tell another story about Sophia Street, where I live. It's about lasting love between friends.

Our indoor-outdoor cat Koi is quite friendly. So, after fourteen years in the neighborhood, he has many friends. Some are other cats. And some are people.

Mrs. L is one of his human friends. She lives two doors down. When Koi was young, she worried about him. She would ring our doorbell to let us know. "It's cold," she would say. "Is your cat home?" Sometimes Koi would be with her. Then she would say, "Hello, it's raining. Your cat is home now."

Young Koi liked jumping and climbing. Sometimes he would leap up on a neighbor's roof. If their upstairs window was open, Koi would walk right in to visit. So, sometimes Mrs. L would come by to tell us, "He was on my ceiling!" Her English isn't perfect, but we knew she was talking about her roof.

Well, Koi is older now. He's lost some weight. We worry about him, too. So we took him to the vet, and ordered every test we could afford. The diagnosis? He's aging.

But, last fall, he suddenly stopped eating for a few days. And we worried about him again. Until we saw this sign up in the neighborhood:

Hello Neighbor! We are trying to locate the owner of this male cat. He is regularly seen on Sophia Street where we live. He comes to our house every day wanting food and hangs out on our back porch.

New neighbors! If they knew Koi, they'd realize: he wanted to *meet* them, not *eat* with them! I called them and explained. Also, I asked what they were feeding him. Turns out, it was a particular treat I hadn't tried.

But back to Mrs. L, star of this story. Mrs. L is aging, too. She is bent over from arthritis. She shuffles when she walks. It's hard for her to walk a flight of stairs—like the one up to our front door.

But one day, about a week ago, the doorbell rang. I opened the door and there was Mrs. L, masked and holding a small bag. "Here's some canned food for Koi. He's getting old. He can't eat the hard food anymore," she says. I tell her he has every kind of food at home. But I also thank her for being Koi's friend, and accept the gift.

Then I close the door and I cry. Mrs. L loves Koi so much. They are aging together. She worries he is feeling what she feels. In fact, she comes by again, and I accept the gift again.

Now, Koi is a very orderly cat. He follows a clear routine. And he insists we follow it too. So, at his request, he goes out for a while every morning. But this week, he did something different. He stayed in for three full days. He had a reason; we just don't know what it is.

Today, the doorbell rang again. It was Mrs. L, with another gift bag. She apologized for forgetting her mask. I tell her again that Koi has plenty of food. "He comes to my house every morning!" she says. "I didn't see him for a few days and I thought he was dead. I worry!"

So, I tell her that we worry, too. That Koi has been to the doctor, twice recently. That the doctor says he is fine. She looks relieved. Also, I tell her that he has every kind of food; we can't accept so many gifts. And, again, I thank her for being Koi's friend. "Okay," she says. And I watch her walk, slowly and with difficulty, back down the stairs.

—— Day 23 ——

Gevurah she'b'Netzach

Judgment within Eternity

Maybe you've heard of hell. Some Christian traditions say it's a possible destination in the afterlife journey. Each Christian's life is judged on the day of their death. Did they turn towards God and let go of sin? Then, they get eternal life in heaven. Did they turn away from God and towards sin? Then they get eternal damnation in hell.[1]

And maybe you've heard of the Day of Judgment. For Muslims, it's the end of the world as we know it. On that day, all people will be judged.[2] Did they follow the path where grace abounds? Then, they get eternal life in paradise. Or did they follow the path of unbelief and anger? Then, some teachers say, they get eternal damnation in hell.[3]

If you take these teachings literally, they are harsh. So, let's look at them a bit less literally, as many Christians and Muslims do, too. One day you will die. Then, you'll have no more chances to fix your mistakes. Whatever you left broken will stay that way. But you don't know when that day will come. It could even be tomorrow. So, go ahead, fix your mistakes today!

1. Talbot, "Heaven and Hell."
2. Zaidi, "Belief in the Day of Judgment."
3. Mir, *Understanding the Islamic Scripture*, Kindle.

Judaism, the tradition that influenced me the most, is a bit less harsh in its teaching. Sure, there is a day of judgment. But it comes every year. We judge ourselves and fix what we can. Then God judges us and decides how our next year will be. That's it! There's no eternal judgment. Just year-by-year judgment.

And when we die? Yes, we are judged. If we are good, integrated, and healthy inside, then we go quickly to the Garden of Eden. But if we aren't, then we spend time in purgatory. And, after a deep inner workout lasting no more than a year, we head on up to the Garden.[4]

Oh, and if we left our loved ones on a bad note? We appear to them in the shape of memories or dreams, every day for the eleven months that they say the mourner's kaddish prayer. Then, every year on the anniversary of our passing. And occasionally, at random times. Gradually, our loved ones let go of bad memories and come to know the newer, purer us.[5]

So—if that's the teaching—why am I so hard on myself? Why can't I let go of self-judgment even after others forgive me? Where does my sense of *eternal judgment* come from?

4. Simcha Paull Raphael, *Jewish Views of the Afterlife.*
5. Duhan-Kaplan, "The Afterlife Journey."

Day 24

Tiferet she'b'Netzach

Beauty within Endurance

Today I'm feeling contrary. So I'd like to talk about the beauty of things that *don't* endure. Like cherry blossoms. And social justice.

Cherry blossoms first. Sophia Street is lined with late-blooming cherry trees. Well, today's their day. Finally! Pink blossoms are popping open like crazy. We may be in a lockdown, but that doesn't stop the cherry-blossom tourists. All day, they come in twos and threes, on foot or by bicycle. And they take pictures of themselves framed in pink.

The blossoms are rare; they last only a few days. That is why people run to see them. And also why I can't stop looking out the window. Through my window, today, the world looks beautiful.

From the outside, though, our house looks a bit different. Yesterday, I noticed two young men discussing the sign in our front window. It says, "End Racism."

For the record: the young men liked the sign. If it were safe, I could have invited them in. Right inside the foyer they would see the "Fight Sexism" sign. Two steps to the left into our living room they would see the "Stronger Than Hate: United Against Antisemitism" sign.

These signs? We held them at vigils and protests. When we look at them, memories of group solidarity uplift us. So, they are powerful symbols. But symbols alone don't bring about change.

Education helps, too. For years, I've tried to do a tiny part as an educator. Education, in fact, takes up almost all my time. But is teaching enough? Are these causes enough? And I am doing enough?

The answer to all three questions—for me—is *No*. It's always No. Because the work is never done. Some battles have to be fought in every generation. Sometimes there is progress. Then, the world becomes more just, and justice saves lives. And, as Jewish and Islamic teachers say, each time we save a single life we save a world of relationships. And that is beautiful.

But justice cannot endure. Not without constant tending. Because there's always someone at hand who prefers a divided community. Hate helps them get profits, power, votes, fame. So they'll stoke racism, sexism, antisemitism. Anytime.[1]

So is any work ever enough? Not really. But that's no reason to stop. Instead, it's a reason to continue.[2]

---

1. Stanley, *Fascism*.

2. As Rabbi Tarfon said in *Pirkei Avot* 2:16, "It's not on you to finish the work, but you're not free to avoid it, either." Translation mine.

─── Day 25 ───

Netzach she'b'Netzach

Eternity within Eternity

*W*hoa. But also: *Hooray!*

Whoa because it's a tangle of abstract ideas. Could there really be different kinds of eternity? Like, a shorter eternity that fits inside a longer one?

Hooray because I love abstract ideas. In fact, I'm sure there are different kinds of eternities.

There's a length of time that feels like forever. Say, three thousand years. Even though that's only thirty Aunt Sylvias ago. (She lived to one hundred.)

And then there's a length of time that goes on forever. Because that's how linear time works.

Finally, there's a way of being outside of time. God, for example, who created time, can't be measured in time.[1]

Three different kinds of eternity. The first is smaller than the second which is smaller than the third. Or something like that.

But also *Hooray* because abstract ideas matter.

At dinner tonight we talked about Canadian politics. Specifically, about big oil. And the ups and downs of Alberta's oil-driven economy.

Then, Eli, our adult son, asked a question. "What do you think about nuclear power? People say it's cost-effective and efficient."

---

1. Ibn Gabirol, *Font of Life*, Part I.

"No," I said. "Hard pass. A single leak can devastate a region."

"No," Charles, my spouse, said. "It generates poisonous waste. What happens when we run out of places to store it safely?"

Suddenly we realized: we might be wrong about the science. But we are right about time. We are doing long-term future thinking. And people rarely do that.

"Most people can imagine their grandchildren, and maybe their great-grandchildren," Eli said. "But not really beyond that."

Whoa. No one takes eternity seriously. Or, to tone down the hyperbole: many people take it too lightly. Maybe, they think, it's an attribute of a God who lives outside of time. But it's got nothing to do with our world. Here, everything's temporary. So, why worry long-term?

So here it is, a challenge. I'll make it easy, based on the shortest kind of eternity. *Can we think thirty Aunt Sylvias ahead?*

—— Day 26 ——

Hod she'b'Netzach

Gratitude within Endurance

Theologically speaking, God is eternal. But humans only temporarily endure.

We're so different.

So, *Hod she'b'Netzach* might mean two entirely different things. One expresses God's nature. The other expresses human nature.

Hod can means glory. *Netzach* can mean Eternity. Then, *hod she'b'netzach* is the glory in eternity. Why is God so glorious? Because, one might answer, God is unique; God is eternal being. Maybe God *is* the *hod she'b'netzach*. (Is that not a wild and wacky definition of God?)

But guess who isn't glorious and eternal? Human beings. The ones whose lives are, as philosopher Thomas Hobbes puts it, nasty, brutish, and short.[1]

What can *hod she'b'netzach* mean for us? *Hod* can also mean gratitude. And *netzach* can also mean endurance. Then, *hod she'b'netzach* would be the gratitude in endurance.

What does it mean for a person to endure? To stay alive? Keep moving forward? With personhood intact? How is gratitude part of that?

1. Hobbes, *Leviathan*, 43.

Could I answer this out of my own experience? Maybe with a little fragment of an answer?

Enduring is an inner conversation between two voices: the "keep going" angel and the "give up" angel. One where the "keep going" angel speaks in a louder voice. What pushes up its volume? Sometimes it's love. Maybe for someone you hope to see again. Or for someone you don't want to disappoint. And then, you're just grateful you have someone to keep you going.

That's me. I'm grateful to have a reason to endure.

Is endurance a taste of eternity? A taste of glory? Yes, if you want to wax poetic. But no, if you want to be realistic. Because the world is full of hard things. And not all of them can be softened with theology.

—— Day 27 ——

Yesod she'b'Netzach

Foundation within Endurance

What is the foundation of a lasting relationship? One foundation is compromise. And, in the Torah, Aaron is the master of compromise.

Aaron's sons Nadab and Avihu die while approaching the altar. It happens in front of thousands of people, during the opening day celebration at the *mishkan,* the traveling wilderness tabernacle. The staff goes into emergency management mode, and the celebration abruptly ends.[1]

Then, some time later, Moses asks Aaron to facilitate a kind of do-over, a huge public ritual to purify the sanctuary. Maybe Moses says, "Brother Aaron, can we design a ritual that acknowledges what happened, but also allows us to move forward?"

So here's the ritual they design. At the altar, in front of thousands of people, Aaron brings forward two goats. And, using a lottery, he randomly decides which goat will die and which goat will live. One goat will become a purification offering, burnt to ashes. The other goat will get away.

The do-ever ritual replays what happened on opening day. Some young priests survived and walked away. Others were burnt.

1. Lev 10.

But the do-over ritual doesn't end there. It keeps going, until one priest launders his clothes and another takes out the garbage.[2]

I imagine this ritual is hard for grieving father Aaron. Maybe he wants to avoid the *mishkan* altogether. But his brother Moses really wants him to serve. So Aaron makes a compromise. He offers one goat on the altar. But he lets the other get away, like he wishes he could.

And maybe—this isn't the most popular interpretation, but it is a valid one—Aaron's late sons wanted to avoid some of the *mishkan's* rituals, too. Maybe, on opening day, they prepared their offering without any meat. So with only oil and spices on the flame, the altar blew up. And then the young men died, protesting the animal offerings. Maybe that's why Aaron refuses to eat his meat offering that day. And why Moses immediately says it's okay for priests to eat meat.

So, with the ritual of the two goats, Aaron makes another compromise. He honours his brother, who wants animal offerings, by offering one goat. And he honours his sons, who protest the offerings, by letting the other goat get away. It's not a perfect compromise, especially not for the goats. But few compromises are perfect.[3]

Compromise is always a work in progress. And I'm making slow progress on several fronts. At home, I compromise on my kitchen rules, since no one wants to follow them. At work, I compromise on inter-religious perspectives, advocating more quietly than I want to. Every time I leave the house, I compromise on public health rules; no two people interpret them the same way. Inside my own conscience, I compromise on just about everything.

True confession: I feel I never get it right. But neither does Aaron, Torah's archetypal peacemaker. Maybe that's the nature of compromise: a juggling act that never ends, a moving foundation for a lasting relationship.

---

2. Lev 16:1–28.

3. Duhan-Kaplan, *Mouth of the Donkey,* 17–22.

──────── Day 28 ────────

Shechinah she'b'Netzach

Presence within Eternity

G od close and far.
   In theological jargon, a close-dwelling God is an "immanent" God.

And the eternal, infinite, omnipresent, omnipotent God—so different from anything in our world—is the transcendent God.[1]

Two facets of the same God. So says the author of the hymn *Adon Olam*. First, the poet describes the transcendent God. This God existed before our world began, and will continue to exist after our world ends. Then, the poet describes a close personal relationship with this same God. "I'm not afraid; as long as I live, God is with me."[2]

Ah, *Adon Olam*. The poet knows our world is flawed. Not every problem can be solved. Many lives won't have happy endings. But God, somehow, can hold it all. We may destroy a family, a neighborhood, a country, a planet. But God will keep on keeping on. And this makes the poet feel safe.

Some days, I love *Adon Olam*. But today, I don't. Today, *Adon Olam* seems backwards to me. Today, I start with immanence, and feel my way towards transcendence. In beautiful ways, but also in painful ways.

---

1. Westphal, "Immanence and Transcendence," Kindle.
2. Duhan-Kaplan, *Infinity Inside*, 109–18.

When I see the spring cherry blossoms, for example, that's beautiful. The pink flowers open my heart, launch my soul, and set it soaring. I don't even have to think about the Eternal One. I just feel It.

But when I see cruelty, that's painful. The victims hurt, the world hurts, my heart hurts. Then, I feel there must be a higher order. One that will break through soon. It's not a conscious thought; it's an immediate yearning.

And when I place the two experiences, beauty and pain, side by side, my heart breaks. Because I feel that God is failing us. How can God be so present in the blossoms, but so absent from the hearts of cruel people?

And then I ask myself: how can I, in good conscience and with a straight face, stand up and teach religion day after day?

Week Five

Hod

—

הוד

Splendor, Gratitude,
Humility

—— Day 29 ——

Chesed she'b'Hod

Love within Splendor

T he love that's part of divine splendor.

It's right there in one of my favorite parts of the Torah.

Moses says to God, "Show me your Presence." God says, "No one can see me and live. But I'll show you what follows me!" So God puts Moses in a safe rocky shelter and then passes by. Someone—God or Moses, the text isn't clear—calls out. "God, compassionate, gracious, patient, full of love and truth!"[1]

Love is a direct revelation of God. It's what we see right after God passes by.

Isn't that obvious?

Well, sometimes it is. Like when I was quite sick a decade ago. Pain had worn down my spirit. So I didn't think much of myself. And I cried, often. Until I remembered: my mother loves me. Not because I am good, or pretty, or smart, or healthy. But just because I exist.[2]

And that's what people mean by divine love. Love beamed your way, simply because you exist. You do nothing to earn it. And you can't lose it.

But sometimes, love doesn't feel divine at all. Because often, when people love, it's not so pure. They love an image of you. And

1. Exod 33:12—34:8.
2. Duhan-Kaplan, *Mysticism in Midlife*.

then, one day, they discover: you don't look like the image at all. So they insist that you change. Because, they feel, you owe them that much. After all, they love you.

Divine love is my ideal.

But I'm not so good at it. Because sometimes the people I love annoy me. Or disappoint me. And then, I want them to change. Yes, change takes work, but I expect them to do it. Why? Because I love them. And thus they should love me. And to show it, they should change.

This is silly, I know. And unrealistic. Maybe even cruel. But it seems hard just to accept everyone as they are. To figure out what to ask for and what to let go.

How can I get better at it?

— Day 30 —

Gevurah she'b'Hod

Boundaries within Splendor

T he tradition of Kabbalah, Jewish mysticism, describes God as infinite energy. So infinite that It fills all space and time. Thus, It leaves no room for anything else.[1]

Except It also holds everything else. So, It's formless, forming, and formed all at the same time.

And, thus, our world is always perched at the moment of creation.[2] The formless energy is forming stuff that is being formed. All the time. And in all the space.

At the right time of day, you can even see creation happening. At dawn, for example. So says Psalm 104. "God, you dress yourself in splendor. Light is your gown, you draw open the heavens like a curtain."[3]

Maybe that's why medieval philosopher Moses Maimonides says (and I paraphrase), "Just look out the window! You'll see proof of the Creator's existence."[4] Because the world is a form that God's splendor takes. Or splendor is a form that God takes. Or both.

Just look out the window, says the argument. See how intricate nature is! How neatly ecosystems move in harmony. Obviously,

1. *Tikkunei Zohar* 122b.

2. Kurzweil, *Kabbalah for Dummies,* 57–62.

3. Ps 104:1–2.

4. Maimonides, *Mishneh Torah, Yesodot HaTorah,* 2:2.

there's a great intelligence at work. It's a mystical version of the "argument from design."[5]

And as long as you see cherry blossoms through the window, the argument works.

But if you see, for example, people harassing, stealing, assaulting each other, the argument fails. Because, obviously, there's a great lack of intelligence at work.

Is this proof of the Creator's existence, too? What form of splendor is it, then?

5. Aquinas, *Summa Theologica*, 1.2.3.

—— Day 31 ——

Tiferet she'b'Hod

Beauty within Splendor

F inding balance through humility.

On the tree of *sefirot*, *tiferet* sits in the middle, like a perfectly balanced heart.

Love and judgment both flow into it.

Hod. What's a perfect balance between the word's two translations, splendor and gratitude? Some say it's humility.

Okay, I'm working on it.

Sometimes I know I'm splendid. I have strong self-esteem. And I do many things well.

But sometimes I'm terrified. Because others depend on me, and I know I failed them. My cat should be healthier, my husband happier, my students' work better.

And then I swing back and forth between these extremes. Confident one day and anxious the next.

Of course my therapist would say, "Draw better boundaries. You are not responsible for other people's inner lives."

Well, that's one way to find balance: be more self-sufficient. But what if there's another way? An exact opposite way.

What if I notice how much I depend on others, too?

Before I eat, for example, I always give thanks to God for feeding me. Sometimes I use the traditional Jewish formula, "Bless you God . . . who brings forth bread from the ground."

But I know the formula is a shorthand. Because a lot goes on before a seed in the ground becomes bread on your table.

Old plants decay in the ground. Insects till the soil. Farmers and investors plan. Workers sow, tend, harvest, in vehicles built by factory workers and maintained by mechanics. Millers turn seed into flour with their machines. Then, someone sells the flour, others ship it, still others bake it in businesses large and small. Finally, I buy it and (ideally) everyone gets back enough money to keep doing their work.

See how important I am? The whole system turns on my little act. And see how unimportant I am, too? I'm just a little cog in a big system.

Yes, my little failings affect the system. But they don't break it. Yes, my contribution makes a difference. But my talents don't uphold the world. And each day I make peace with this balance.

—— Day 32 ——

Netzach she'b'Hod

Endurance within Humility

S uccessful humility.
      Or, in other words, a good public persona.[1]

Sometimes, I do think about my persona. I'm a local person, but I'm also a public person. I'm a parent. And I write, speak, teach, organize, lead things, help a bit with pastoral care. So, I know *a lot* of people.

To some of them, I'm a role model. And I'm okay with that.

But I'm also just me.

So, what kind of public persona should I aim for?

I'm kind of torn, actually.

On the one hand, I'm reserved. I'd like to appear dignified and graceful. Speak briefly and to the point. Just the right words at the right time. If I make a mistake, I'll fix it. But I don't need to explain why I do or don't do every little thing.

On the other hand, I'm friendly and funny. Cynical, sardonic, realistic. And, when I'm not holding back, I'm compassionate. So, sometimes I want people to know that I get it. I've felt pain, too. Known depression, grief, failure, anger. So, it's important for me to talk about those things. Teach and write about them.

But how can I do both? Be reserved and open at the same time?

---

1. Jung, *Two Essays*, Kindle.

Here's one thing I've tried.

While I'm working out my distress, I keep quiet. Because I don't want to look confused. And I certainly don't want to burden anyone with my confusion!

But once I've settled something inside myself, then I feel free to talk about it. In a way that I think could be helpful to others, of course.

Still, I wonder. Am I honest about the reasons I hold my worries close? Or is there more? Do I try, sometimes, to protect people who hurt me? Or protect myself from their wrath if I embarrass them? When are those the right goals—and when not?

— Day 33 —

Hod she'b'Hod

Splendor within Splendor

What is something simple, personal, and real that's a perfect blend of splendor, gratitude, and humility? Here's an idea: choosing a *role model*. Someone you think is splendid, whose life or work you're grateful for. You aspire to be like them. Even though, in your humility, you know you aren't yet.

I've admired and copied many role models. In every activity I do! But most of the time I do it unconsciously. Instead of thinking "I admire this person," I just get busy learning from them. So, some of my role models may never know how much they have influenced me. Heck, I may never know. And thus, I might not even say "thank you."

Today, day 33 of the *omer*, is *Lag ba'Omer!* It's holiday with a humble name: "33rd day of the *omer*." It's also a holiday of mysterious origins. It seems to recall the second Judean revolt against Roman occupation (132 CE). And it seems to celebrate the intellectual heroes of the resistance. Like Rabbi Shimon bar Yochai. And, speaking of role models, Rabbi Akiva.

Scholars have sketched a timeline of Rabbi Akiva's life. But it's hard to separate fact from legend. For example, Akiva's name is an Aramaic variation on *Yakov,* Jacob. And, according to legend, Akiva's life is a variation on Jacob's. Jacob falls in love with Rachel, works as a shepherd for seven years in order to marry her, then works another seven to appease her father. Finally, Jacob even impresses Rachel's father with his skilled sheep breeding. Akiva works as a shepherd, falls in love with the boss's daughter Rachel, then studies for seven years to impress her. And then he studies another seven years. And, finally, he shows Rachel's nasty father how competent he is.

So, it makes sense to honor Akiva as a kind of second Jacob. The first Jacob is an early spiritual ancestor of the Jewish people. Akiva is a spiritual ancestor of modern Judaism. He lived through the destruction of the Temple and the birth of Christian mission. True, he didn't work alone. But, without him, Judaism might not have found a future.

What, specifically, did he do? He organized all the early rabbinic teachings about law and custom. He put them in logical categories and arranged them in logical order. Yes, he created the oral Mishna. He explored mysticism, yet integrated it with his rational side. Also, he encouraged close reading of the Torah. Every detail counts, he said! So keep reading with fresh eyes and spinning creative interpretations. Not just about law and practice, but about love and legend, too.

Love, he taught, is the Torah's most important message. If we love, suffering can point us towards the future. And towards others, too, so we can help them, financially and spiritually.[1]

Yes, Rabbi Akiva is my role model. We share some skills. We're both intellectual and mystical; both close readers of Torah. Hopeful we can impress our partners. That's why I'm drawn to Rabbi Akiva.

But I don't share all his skills. And those are the ones I aspire to. Seeing love in everything. Finding meaning in suffering. Being hopeful about the future. And knowing how to practice justice.

1. Hammer, *Akiva.*

— Day 34 —

Yesod she'b'Hod

Foundation within Splendor

Where do the names of the *sefirot* come from?

Apparently, King David first listed them. So the story goes, anyway. With great ceremony, David commissioned his son Solomon to build the Temple. In front of an audience, David praised God. "To you God, belongs judgment, beauty, eternity, and splendor—*gevurah, tiferet, netzach,* and *hod*—because of everything in heaven and on earth!" Then, David asked the audience to donate generously to the building project.[1]

Yes, I'm cynical about the motives of kings. But I recognize: this was a special day for King David. A day of heightened spiritual perception, when one might actually see the divine at work. So, following David's lead, I see the *sefirot* as attributes of God. And I also see them as interfaces. Places where our human experience reaches towards something divine.

It's easy to see this with the *sefirah* of splendor. Here, I adapt an example from sixteenth-century philosopher Judah Abrabanel. Imagine looking up at the sky on a peaceful day. Maybe it's a night sky full of stars. Or a daytime sky, blue with fluffy clouds. The splendid sight overwhelms us. We feel full, maybe we ache a bit, too. And we start to think: how vast the universe must be![2]

1. 1 Chr 29:11.
2. Abrabanel, *Philosophy of Love,* III.

If sight is not your thing, imagine a beautiful smell. The song of a favorite bird. Or any time a bodily sense showed you something splendid, and filled you with so much wonder your body couldn't process it all. So, a little door opened in your mind. And you began to think about your experience, to try to understand it. Ordinary perception pushed you to a higher kind of perception.

Right now, I'm yearning for these little interfaces. I need to see the big things in the little things. So I try, every afternoon, when my spouse and I take a walk to the community garden. My husband inspects the little fruit trees. Are the buds opening? The leaves healthy? Meanwhile, I wander through the flowers with my phone camera, capturing bursts of orange, purple, yellow, red. I look at each photo, editing as I go. How can I crop this photo, so that it is even more splendid? So that looking at the photo becomes an amazing sensory experience? A prompt for opening onto higher perception? So that I see not just a flower, but the divine attribute of splendor itself?

True confession: these new flower photos are the exact same ones I took last spring. But please do not laugh at me. These are not mere photos. They are, rather, snapshots of spiritual practice, gateway moments to the divine. And they remind me: splendor can be a foundation for spiritual perception.

—— Day 35 ——

Shechinah she'b'Hod

Presence within Splendor

Shechinah isn't just any divine Presence. *Shechinah* is like the presence of a loving mother. One who—as the Talmud says—follows you into exile.[1] Physical exile, but also spiritual exile. Emotional exile. She cries for you and with you. And then, she pleads with God to bring you home.[2] Because you've suffered enough. And because home, once you get there, will be a splendid place. A place without pain or fear or sadness.

Our cat Koi is in "home hospice care" now. That's what I call it, anyway. Our vet can't treat him. He's not eating anymore. Just sipping a bit of water every few hours. He can walk only a few steps; then he rests. So we set him up in the living room. He's got a little station with water, litter, and a box he can hide in. He purrs and we pet him. We whisper that we love him. Then he purrs some more.

Soon, we believe, he will be in a splendid place. Exactly what that place is, we don't know. Probably not a heaven filled with angels. Not a garden of Torah scholars, either. And definitely not the edge of a rainbow bridge, where he frolics with his sister Keely and his friend Auto. Because Koi's true home is not really a place. It's more of a way of being.

1. *b. Megillah* 29a.
2. *Lamentations Rabbah*, 24.

Koi is made of organic chemicals plus . . . . We don't know what the "plus" is. Spirit, soul, or spark, maybe. But we see it whenever we see Koi. Soon its way of being will change, too. And then we'll see it only with our spiritual perception. It will touch our feelings, dreams, and memories.

We are Koi's family. So, we will journey with Koi as far as we can. After that, it's up to *Shechinah*. She will bring him home. And she'll dwell with him there, too. Because she is his real mother.

Week Six

Yesod

———

יסוד

Foundation, Grounding

—— Day 36 ——

Chesed she'b'Yesod

Love within Foundation

We all know love is a foundation. Children need it to thrive. It helps them feel secure as they explore and learn. Then, they don't see the world as a threat and, defensively, turn on everyone they meet.

Adults need love too. Because, at any age, neglect and abuse are devastating.

And there are so many ways life could go wrong. I'm doing some research right now for a paper on trauma-informed teaching.[1] I think graduate theological education can be healing. But only if we know what we're doing.

So I read about inter-generational trauma. Sometimes harm is done to a community, and its support systems are damaged, too. Then, individual healing is hard. And victims may lash out at one another.[2]

I read about moral injury, where people, caught up in a system, harm others. They don't know how to live with what they did. And they can't easily find guidance on how to atone.[3]

1. Duhan-Kaplan, "Healing Social Trauma."
2. Methot, *Legacy,* 35–38.
3. Firestone, *Wounds into Wisdom,* 87–93.

And I read about spiritual abuse, too. Someone turns to a trusted spiritual teacher for advice and support, but instead gets rejected and blamed. Sometimes even manipulated or exploited.[4]

In my life, I have tried not to injure other people. Surely, though, I've made some mistakes. Passed on family trauma. Identified with an abusive group. Misunderstood my pastoral role. Surely family systems and social networks have drawn me into things that are so big, I can't yet see them.

Often, I worry about the things I can see. Some of them are little failures. Like the time my very young son didn't get what he wanted. So he stomped and yelled. And I said "Don't be angry!" Then I thought better of it and said, "It's okay to feel angry but please stop yelling." Twenty years later, I still wonder: did I crush his ability to feel?

Or the time my very young daughter and I walked past a hornet's nest. "Let's run!" I said, and grabbed her hand. But then a hornet zoomed our way. I got distracted and dropped her hand. "Come on!" I said, "Follow me!" And then, ashamed, I took her hand again. To this day, I still wonder: did I teach her to feel unsafe in the world?

So, as you see, I want to love fully. I have high standards. But I can only see what I know how to see. Thus, I can only name my small mistakes. For now, anyway; I hope I'm learning.

4. Johnson and VanVonderen, *Spiritual Abuse,* 20–21.

––––– Day 37 –––––

Gevurah she'b'Yesod

Judgment within Foundation

I deally, says Aristotle, good judgment is a habit.[1] And—I add—
ideally, you learned it gradually. First, your elders made judgments for you. Then, they gave you advice. They caught you when
you fell. And finally, at age forty, your good habits were in place.[2]

Well, I've been over forty for two decades now. By forty, I
had some good habits of judgment. But now, at sixty, I'm finally
starting to trust them.

Around procrastination, for example. Sometimes, when
there's an academic task on my desk, I avoid it. Why? I'm pretty
sure I'm not lazy.

Usually, it turns out I'm just not ready. My subconscious
mind hasn't yet done its work. It hasn't organized or integrated
the information yet. So, if I tried to work, I'd just be "spinning my
wheels," so to speak.

However, my subconscious rarely explains this clearly. Instead, it just doesn't push up any creative energy. So I look at the
project and, well, I just feel tired. A little lethargic. And then, a
little guilty.

1. Aristotle, *Nicomachean Ethics* 1103a-b.

2. Adulthood begins at age forty according to Pythagoras, as represented
by Laërtius, *Lives of the Philosophers* 342, § 7.

Until I remember: you've been here before, Laura. Your creative process has its own time and its own wisdom. Trust your judgment.

Sometimes I avoid a task because no one really needs me to do it. Let's say it's an interpersonal task that puts me in the middle between two other people. I'll avoid it, then dread it, because I know it will feel bad. And then I'll quietly call myself a coward. But then, when I do nothing, magic happens. People talk to each other directly. Or, their strong feelings fade and they move on. Because the thing wasn't really so important to them, anyway.

And then I realize: that's why I avoided the task. My subconscious mind knew my meddling wasn't helpful. It directed the process. But, again, it forgot to explain what it was doing. So I felt myself a failure.

Even though by now I should know: sometimes, I can trust my judgment.

— Day 38 —

Tiferet she'b'Yesod

Balance within Foundation

Where is the point of balance? Where do our bodies find their foundation?

In ballet class, I learned: *balance is up.* You stand on strong feet. Then you lift up through your legs, torso, chest. Your eyes look up, too. And when you rise on your toes, you lengthen your whole body upwards. It's foolproof. You will never fall.

Years later, I took a singing class. The teacher wanted us to breathe into our hips. To feel our voice moving through our whole bodies, not just through our chests. So, he said: *balance is down.* Ground yourself, and you will never lose your voice.

Finally, I learned to teach hatha yoga. Every standing movement, I taught, flows from the mountain pose.[1] "A mountain is rooted in the ground," I would say. "And it reaches up to the sky. So, from the hips down, lengthen your body towards the ground. And from the hips up, lengthen towards the sky." *Balance is a balance of up and down.*

Well, I don't really know how to find balance. So, I think I'll just keep moving.

---

1. Iyengar, *Light on Yoga,* 63–64.

---— Day 39 ——-

Netzach she'b'Yesod

Endurance within Foundation

H istory doesn't repeat. But—as the famous saying goes—it does rhyme.[1]

So the present isn't exactly like the past. But it does hold a few echoes. A few things that sound alike.

When I listen for the rhymes, I feel I'm practicing "historical imagination."

Sure, people lived differently in the past. They had different ideas, different cultures. *But they had exactly the same human nature.* For example, some were greedy; others were generous.

As a child, I learned about some great ancient civilizations. Egypt built pyramids; Babylonia mastered astronomy; Greece developed philosophy and theatre.

Then, as young adult, I learned about the Enlightenment, a modern movement to bring science, literacy, and critical philosophy back to Europe.

So, I wondered, where did all the knowledge go? During these so-called "dark ages"?

But now I know. Or, at least, I have a theory, based on what I see today.

Some people deliberately suppressed knowledge. Because they could make more money if others were ignorant.

1. Colombo, *Neo Poems*, 46.

And some deliberately suppressed science. Because they could make more money if others scrabbled through life.

They talked trash and spread hate. So people would see each other as enemies. And then not compare notes.

And they encouraged people to enjoy violence. To find it exciting, even. So they could easily get mobs and militias to fight for their profits.

We're entering a new dark age.

But I try not to despair.

Because I still hope there is more good than evil in the world. Why? Well, no one has destroyed the whole world yet. Somehow, it endures.

Love, education, solidarity, spirituality can be a solid foundation. *As long as enough people practice them.*

— Day 40 —

Hod she'b'Yesod

Gratitude within Foundation

Caretaking. A hidden foundation of the world. One that merits much gratitude.[1] But gets little.

What shall I do with myself today? I'm not sure what day it is. I know I haven't slept in three.

My chest hurts. For a week, nothing except Koi-cat has been real. Oh, I cooked. I worked at my job. But none of that counted.

Mostly I wanted to love as fiercely and deeply as I could. To cram five years of love into five days. Be a caretaker for Koi and his fragile body.

My son took the day shifts. I took the night shifts. We soothed Koi when he cried out. Followed him when he wobbled to a new position. Offered him water. Gave him space when we thought he was safe. Held him when he took his last breaths.

But today, my son is back to work. So I make my own rituals. I wash the towels Koi soiled in his last days. Then, I unfold the soft bed of blankets I made to cushion his distended body. I clean his litter box. Hide the cat food, stash away the cat bowls. It's not that I want to forget. It's just healing to touch his things.

Caretaking is exhausting. It's messy. And it can be the purest expression of love. But I was grateful to do it.

---

1. Duhan-Kaplan, "Ethic of Care."

My husband prepared Koi's grave. After we buried Koi, my husband planted a hosta lily in the dirt. The rabbis say burying the dead is the purest mitzvah. Because you don't expect the dead to give you anything in return.[2] Well that's what caretaking is like, too.

You don't get recognition. There's no celebrity in caretaking. But you do weave the invisible safety net that holds the world.

And yes, I know our support for Koi was easy. At least, on the scale of human challenges. So, I want to celebrate the quiet care people give one another in hard times.

2. Lamm, *Jewish Way in Death and Mourning.*

—— Day 41 ——

Yesod she'b'Yesod

Foundation within Foundation

What kind of foundation is this ultimate foundation?

Not the solid one we see under a house. But a dynamic one, a liquid one, always on the move.

Maybe you have a little carafe where you mix your salad dressing. You put in oil, vinegar, salt, pepper, sugar. Then you shake it up. And, when you're done, you have something new that will bring your salad to life.

Yesod, some say, is like the little carafe. It holds the energies of the five upper *sefirot*. It blends them into something new.[1] Then, it passes them on to *Shechinah*. She will bring the spiritual energies into the world. And her spiritual presence will bring people a deeper life.

Or maybe you read Dr. Seuss's book *McElligot's Pool*. It's in the news now because the Seuss Foundation won't publish its racist artwork or allusions anymore. But maybe the book's premise can stand alone.

A child stands over a little pond, fishing. He imagines it leads to an underground stream. And the stream flows through the whole world. So, the child knows he is not just randomly fishing his way through life. Instead, he's connected with something truly great.

---

1. Dubov, *The Sefirot*.

Yesod, some say, is like the underground stream. It is a spiritual energy that runs through everything and everyone, connecting us all.

It might be hard to believe this stream exists. It's even harder to perceive it. Think of it this way. In theory, the upper *sefirot* are more subtle. But, really, they are easier to see. Love, clarity, beauty, eternity, splendor are in our actions, our thoughts, and our relationships. And also in nature.

But the foundation? The hidden stream? The spiritual energy of the world? Not so easy to see.

─── Day 42 ───

Shechinah she'b'Yesod

Presence within Foundation

God's maternal presence. Mother of the whole world. Our foundation, so to speak.

So, this happened to me about two years ago: I am walking on campus of the University of British Columbia. It's early afternoon on a damp, grey day. Soon, I have to be in class, so I'm in a bit of a hurry. Two young Korean women, university students, approach me. Each one is holding a Bible. *Oh crap,* I think. *Fundamentalist Christian missionaries.*

"Excuse me," they say, "Do you have a minute?"

"Yes," I say. "But only a minute." I imagine I'm smiling kindly.

"We would like to prove to you," they say, "that God is a woman."

Whoa, I think. *Not your typical missionaries!* Now I'm intrigued. And I'm really smiling. Because I definitely have more than a minute for *this* conversation!

They open their Bible to the beginning. "Look," they say, "at the beginning of Genesis. The Bible says, 'the spirit of God hovers over the waters.'[1] And the Hebrew for 'hovering' is a female word!"

How they know this, I'm not sure. Because the Bible they are holding is a contemporary English translation.

1. Gen 1:1.

"Now, look at this!" they say. And they flip to the end of their Bible, to the final verses of the Book of Revelation. "It says, 'The spirit and the Bride say, come!'[2] So, the spirit of God is female. That proves God is a woman."

Technically, the verses speak in poetry; they don't prove anything. Still, I get the students' point. The Bible begins and ends with God's feminine spirit. She births the world, and she calls it into maturity. Everything else has to be read in light of these two bookends.

But I don't say either of those things. I don't correct or re-state what they said.

Instead, I say, "Let me show you something, too!" And I flip to the Book of Proverbs, chapter 8.

"Look," I say. "It says wisdom is a woman. And that wisdom was with God before creation. As a nanny, a designer, a playful friend."[3]

We talk for about twenty minutes. Then, I give them my business card. I tell them they would love the Vancouver School of Theology.

Then, I walk back to class, dancing a little, and smiling a lot.

Because the young women are brave and radical. They are part of the World Mission Society Church of God, a Korean church that believes in God the Mother. But, here on campus, God the Father rules. No one speaks of the divine mother. But these women hear her calling, anyway.

2. Rev 22:17.

3. Prov 8:22–31.

Week Seven

Shechinah (Malchut)

שכינה (מלכות)

Cosmic Mother, Presence, Royalty

Day 43

Chesed she'b'Shechinah

Love within the Cosmic Mother

M y mother Ruthie was a cosmic force. Brilliant and bizarre. And completely unafraid of death.

The philosopher Plato said: a person who loves wisdom is not afraid of death. Why? Because wisdom is a search for knowledge. Thus, a wise person is aware of what they do and don't know. And, having never died, they don't know what death is like. So, they don't imagine that death is bad for the deceased. And they don't waste energy being afraid of a fantasy.[1]

One day, a man was shot on our street. My mother grabbed a towel and ran out the front door—towards the gunfire. Yes, she was trained in both first aid and firearms. But that wasn't relevant. She didn't think, "It's dangerous, but I know what to do." Instead, she just thought, "someone needs help."

She didn't bring her dog out that day. But she usually had a dog with her. Actually, she usually had four or five dogs. Mom specialized in helping lost dogs. And she ran an informal animal shelter in her tiny urban backyard. No neighbor ever complained, because Mom befriended all of them. Mom did not believe in euthanizing pets; after all, she would not euthanize a human. So, she cared for every dog herself at home until its last breath.

---

1. Plato, *Apology,* 29a–b.

Mom told us when she was ready to die. "My body is giving out," she said. A week later, we sat with her in a hospital. She made jokes with her facial expressions, whispered a little conversation, and smiled at us. Early the next morning, she asked the nurse for a little morphine. Then, Mom fell asleep, and a few moments later, she let go.

Plato is right about a lot of things. But he is wrong about my mom. Mom was unafraid of death, but not because she loved wisdom. Mom was unafraid because she loved. Period. She loved us, her dogs, and, literally, the stranger in the street. Her love crowded out her fear. And thus, she expressed what some spiritual teachers call the highest, most cosmic kind of love. Did it come easily to her, or did she work to develop it? I imagine it's a little bit of both.

Day 44

Gevurah she'b'Shechinah

Judgment within the Cosmic Mother

Somehow, as a mother, I made a few good judgments. But I am not sure how.

One of my young children, for example, was not very focused. So, I made sure to give them only one instruction at a time. For years!

Yes, eventually they grew up. And now they excel at complex strategy games and programming projects.

Another of my young children was rather impulsive. Spoke their mind and did what they wanted to do. But I made a decision never to embarrass them. So, when they were rude or inappropriate, I whispered my instructions into their ear. And they always responded well.

Eventually this child grew up too. Now they have immaculate manners and a gracious way of speaking and writing.

Really, I don't know how I made these good judgments. The only Mom school I went to was the school of being Ruthie's daughter. And she was, let's be honest, a jagged combination of wise and falling apart. Somehow I absorbed the wisdom and left most of the pain behind.

Somehow I was lucky.

Lately, I've been reading about different kinds of trauma. Each has its own definition. But here is one factor shared by most. *In a traumatic experience, your internal resources can't cope with external stressors.*[1]

Somehow, I had the internal resources to cope. A lucky combination of intellect and temperament. As a child, I did not understand how it works. But as a young mother, I had a half-conscious understanding. A child's nervous system is easily overwhelmed. So, I tried not to overwhelm the two children entrusted to me.

Not every child has the resilience I had. Some grow up and only then work painstakingly to learn to love, see others clearly, and handle their own emotions.

I like to imagine that my own resilience was a gift from *Shechinah,* the divine mother. I imagine that she steps in when real mothers and their children struggle. But I also know that is not really true. So, I pray that it will be.

---

1. Prideaux, "How to Heal."

--------- Day 45 ---------

Tiferet she'b'Shechinah

Balance within Presence

F inding a balanced political perspective. It takes enormous presence of mind.

But what if all that is present to my mind is, "I don't know what to say about the news?" Do I *have* to take a social media stand?

Sometimes I get my news from twitter.

But let me clarify that. I *don't* mean that I accept reports from random twitterati.

I *do* mean that I peek at which news stories my friends are sharing. And I also peek at the comments my friends write. That updates me on a different kind of news: what my friends think.

This week, many twitter friends are writing about the violence in Jerusalem. They're not really sharing many news stories. But they are sharing their comments. And many of those comments are slogans.

And I sort of get that, I do.

Most of my friends are not in Jerusalem.

Some work for advocacy organizations. And thus they have to present their organization's position. They say, for example, "The other side must end the terror."

Others are media personalities who spin every news story around the theme they're selling—whether it actually connects or not. So they say, for example, "This is Trump's fault."

Some friends have very little information about history or politics. But they identify strongly with a group. And thus they feel threatened. So they defend their group and blame another.

And many are heartbroken for friends or family in the region. So, they don't know what to say, except, "End the Violence."

Of course I have my own views. I blame the regional tyrants and aspiring tyrants, of all nationalities. They all excel at creating crisis and then pretending to fix it. If other people lose life, health, livelihood, or home, they don't care. As long as they gain a bit more power and—let's be honest—money.

But that's often my go-to perspective. On almost any news story. Because I see it happening almost everywhere.

One thing I wish for right now is to see differently. To have the presence of mind not to default to my usual take. But to balance it with other perspectives.

And I also want the violence and exploitation to end. So I pray for peace.

Day 46

Netzach she'b'Shechinah

Eternity within Presence

I think about the afterlife sometimes, about life after death. I've had some visions of it.[1] So I know? believe? hope? it's another kind of life. One that goes on forever.

When my father died, my son was five years old. One day, about a month after the funeral, my son and I were sitting on the floor playing. My thoughts wandered, my feelings followed. And I began to cry. "Don't worry, Mom," my son said. "Grandpa's soul is part of God now."

My son, now grown, does not remember saying this. So, he can't really tell me what he meant. But I imagine he intuited exactly what my visions show.

When I say "visions of the afterlife," I don't mean dreams. Yes, I have those, too, dreams where precious family members visit. Sometimes those dreams are numinous. That is, they are full of deep feeling and a sense of spiritual presence.

But the visions are different. The most powerful one came a few years ago. It was a new perception of reality that lasted for five hours. A spiritual perception of the essence of consciousness, a quality shared by everything that exists. Among other things, I

---

1. Duhan-Kaplan, "Afterlife Journey."

saw: of course there is life after death, because the source of life does not die.[2]

Last week I had another vision. At first, I thought it was a dream, but a dream expert corrected me.

That night, I was sleeping on the floor, near my ailing cat Koi. He was curled under the rocking chair. At some point I woke up. I saw that he had moved a few feet, and was now curled up against my body.

"Unusual!" I thought. "He's not a cuddly cat. But he wants comfort, and he can only walk a few steps now. So I shouldn't be surprised."

Then Koi began to tremble. I felt him vibrate against my body. Then he started to vibrate faster. And I started to vibrate. And I felt his energy fill my body. When the vibration stopped, I understood. He had transferred his life energy into me.

Then, I looked again. There he was, still curled up under the chair.

Of course there is an afterlife. It's another kind of life. A life of energy. And it goes on forever, because the source of life does not die.

2. Duhan-Kaplan, *Mouth of the Donkey,* 52–55; Duhan-Kaplan, "Vibration of the Other," 124–25.

—— Day 47 ——

Hod she'b'Shechinah

Splendor within Presence

J ust as Shabbat begins, says the *Zohar, tiferet* and *Shechinah* make love. For just a moment, all cosmic forces are in alignment.[1] The world is as perfect as it was at sunset on the sixth day of creation. Each creature is safe and secure in the world's great ecosystem. So, we can pause our efforts to reshape the system, and trust it to heal itself. It's an idealistic vision, I know. But it is the Kabbalistic theory of Shabbat. Once a week, *Shechinah,* our spiritual mother, visits her lover. She visits us, too, and we let her hold us.

I love Shabbat. Just before dinner, I set out Aunt Sylvia's candlesticks. They look like a splendid pair of silver trees, decorated with pomegranates and roses. Sylvia said they belonged to her grandmother and then to her mother. Both of these ancestors died long before I was born. But, whenever I use these candle holders, I feel like my spiritual grandmothers are in the room. And I wonder about them. What did they look like? What did they feel when they lit the candles?

Then, I put the candles in the candlesticks, light them, and say the blessing. And I wonder about the flames, too. Torah says the first creature was light.[2] Did it look like this splendid candle light? A pulsating rainbow of blue, orange, yellow, white, and

1. *Zohar* 2:135a–b.
2. Gen 1:3.

grey? Or did it not look like light at all? Is light just a metaphor for divine energy?

Kabbalists often describe creation as an emanation of divine light. Divine energy flows as spiritual light. It takes conceptual form as intellectual light. It moves in us as emotional light. And it appears in its densest, most easily grasped form as physical light.[3] So you can find this light at every level of consciousness: in sensation, emotion, cognition, and pure spiritual presence; in memory and imagination, too.

Lighting Shabbat candles only takes a few minutes. But what a splendid few minutes it is. Because it also opens a door into timeless realms. I go back 150 years to visit with my grandmothers. 5,700 years to witness the creation story. Beyond time to energies that somehow existed before creation. And, if I am lucky, traces of this journey will stay with me for all twenty-five hours of Shabbat.

3. Schneur Zalman, *Tanya* 36.

—— Day 48 ——

Yesod she'b'Shechinah

Foundation within Royal Presence

The traditional language of Jewish prayer calls God "king." Some people recoil from this. We don't want a king, thank you. Not even a benevolent dictator. We're trying to get rid of tyrants, not worship them!

But some of those same people are comfortable speaking of the world as "God's kingdom." Here, we're all citizens. And we all work together through citizen diplomacy. We try to make the world a better place.[1]

Activism is on my mind this week. At work, we're making final preparations for an online conference on "Religion and Thoughtful Activism." So, today I met with students who will participate in the conference. It looks like we have much in common. We're all interested in practical theology, not just in ideas. We find critical social analyses helpful. We aspire towards radical love for all, though we fall short daily. Also, we believe we have obligations towards Creator and creation. And we are all seeking the best way to fulfill them.

Especially me. Because I often feel I don't know what to do. And, when I do know, I don't do enough. I don't fulfill my responsibility as a citizen of this earthly kingdom. So, even though I believe democracy is better than monarchy, I don't always act

1. Duhan-Kaplan, *Infinity Inside*, 85–88.

that way. Instead, I rely on God to be a good king, who will sort things out for us.

And then I hear the voice of my mother shouting from an upstairs window. She says, "Come on, guys! Do you really believe that your personal inner *tikkun* is enough to change the world? Surely not!"

My mother was not a Talmudic scholar, but if she were, she might say this. The earliest rabbis issued legal rulings they called *takkanot,* corrections, to stop abuses of vulnerable people, especially women and poor men.[2] Surely, they had these rulings in mind when they spoke the words of the *Aleinu* prayer. "We put our hope in you, God, *l'taken olam b'malchut Shaddai*—that you will correct the world through your divine rule." Surely, they saw themselves as the kingdom's activists and advocates. Surely, they would agree: *tikkun olam* is a practice of heart, mind, and action. You do whatever you can.

Sometimes I falter. But my mother? She would be sure.

2. Danan, "Beyond Tikkun Olam."

Day 49

Shechinah she'b'Shechinah

Shechinah within Shechinah

When I was in high school, I took a character photo of my friend Susi. I can't remember where we were—maybe at a cooperative community press office printing our underground newspaper? We found an odd wooden chair. Its frame was intact, but its seat was missing. Susi sat in the chair, adjusted her hat, and grinned. I snapped a photo with two great focal points: her face looking at the camera and her bottom falling through the chair's open frame. Susi's face is alive with energy—so much energy that part of her overflows the chair's frame, reaching down towards the earth. It's surprising, it's funny, it's beautiful.

I remember Susi when I look at the diagram of the *sefirot*, showing the chain of emanation of divine energy into the world. First come the subtle *sefirot*, then the intellectual ones, the emotional ones, and the denser, foundational ones. Finally, there is *Shechinah*, seated on this open-ended throne of energy, pouring it all out into the world, giving birth to things surprising and beautiful.

What is being born in me? At the end of these forty-nine days of reflection? After all, my psyche is part of the flow of divine energy. The archetype of the Cosmic Mother lives inside me, too. What is she birthing? And how will I know? I can't see her directly; she hides in my unconscious. But sometimes, she shows up. Or, at least, comfort, presence, and practical wisdom show up—out of nowhere. But maybe they've been growing inside me for a long time. And now they are being born.

But what is being born right now? In truth, I don't know. I still love my children, grieve my friends, hide behind my persona, and wish God was more of an activist. All I did was bring these truths into the presence of *Shechinah*. So, I'll wait to see what comes next.

Ten Commandments, Inner Edition

Exodus 20:1–15

It's my fiftieth day on this journey of *Sefirat ha'Omer*. But, in Jewish tradition, we don't call it "day 50." We call it *Shavuot*, which means "weeks." Originally, *Shavuot* was a harvest holiday. Later, it became a celebration of revelation, a re-enactment of a numinous experience: hearing the voice of God at Mt. Sinai. One key *Shavuot* ritual is reading the Ten Commandments.

Obviously, the Ten Commandments is an activist document. It is a visionary charter for an ethical and spiritual community. But it also asks us to change our inner states. Sometimes it says so explicitly, telling us to "honor," "remember," and "not covet." But mostly, it quietly invites us to work on the inner change we need in order to change our behavior. And now, after seven weeks of *cheshbon hanefesh*, soul-accounting, inner dimensions of the Ten Commandments come forward for me.

What do the Ten Commandments say to me right now? About the inner resources I have, and the inner *tikkun* I need to make?

(1) *I am YHVH your God.* Often I hear morning birds, or see treetops through a window. Then, I feel I know the Creator. And then I know I have someone I can turn to.

(2) *Don't make idols and worship them.* Often I am down on myself for not achieving something. And sometimes, that's because I measure myself by an unrealistic standard. I have made

something up about myself, and let that fiction control me. Once I realize this, I can begin to break free of an idol.

(3) *Don't take God's name in vain.* Occasionally, I hold a political view so tightly that I believe my idea is God's intention for the universe. When I notice this, then I can loosen my grip just enough to listen thoughtfully to other voices.

(4) *Remember Shabbat and keep it holy.* Every week, busy-busy me wonders why I am so tired on Saturday afternoon. I can't accomplish anything; I can't even hold the book I hoped to read. Then, I remember it's Shabbat, and I understand: rest is my holy work, too.

(5) *Honour your father and mother.* Every few years, I understand more deeply that my parents were just very young humans with good intentions, bumbling their way through the world. And then I have another opportunity to choose to forgive them (or not). In this way, among others, I honor them.

(6) *Do not murder.* Sometimes I remember my father's saying that "a government's first priority is to keep itself in business." Then I remember that governments often neglect people, so I start to learn what I can do to help people live.

(7) *Do not commit adultery.* Sometimes, when I review my family memories, I understand more deeply what caused fractures in my family of origin. And then I try to learn new ways of being that strengthens family love.

(8) *Do not steal.* In my naïve moments, I like to believe that the earth has infinite resources, and my share is infinite too—so if I have a credit card I can get anything I want. And then I realize I don't even need what I want. And maybe I don't even need the money I was about to spend on it. So I donate it to someone who does.

(9) *Do not bear false witness.* Sometimes I realize how much of what I think I "know" isn't knowledge at all. It's just a parroting of what I have read or heard. Then I resolve not to repeat it, and, instead, to deepen my knowledge.

(10) *Do not envy what others have.* All around me, I see successful people. But, sometimes, instead of feeling happy for them, I am suspicious. They only succeeded, I think, because they cheated.

And then, I realize, I am not looking at their success at all. Instead, I see only my own sadness, and disappointment in myself. And I amplify that into anger. So I pray to be released from hurtful directions of thought that cause hurtful action.

These ten habits of self-awareness help me—especially when our social fabric is unraveling and I am fraying, too. Then, I can pause, to make an inner *tikkun*, untangling challenges intentionally, one thread at a time.

Bibliography

Abrabanel, Judah. *The Philosophy of Love* (*Dialoghi d'Amore*). Translated by F. Friedeberg-Seeley and Jean H. Barnes. London: Soncino, 1937.

Aristotle. *Metaphysics*. Translated by C. D. C. Reeve. Indianapolis: Hackett, 2016.

———. *Nicomachean Ethics*. Translated by Robert C. Bartlett and Susan D. Collins. Chicago: University of Chicago Press, 2012.

Bachelard, Gaston. *The Poetics of Space*. Translated by Maria Jolas. Boston: Beacon, 1994.

Bahá'í Community of Canada. "Advancing the Conversation on Reconciliation." In *Spirit of Reconciliation*, edited by Ray Aldred and Laura Duhan-Kaplan, 68–74. Toronto: Canadian Race Relations Foundation, 2020.

Bernhard, Toni. *How to Be Sick: A Buddhist-Inspired Guide for the Chronically Ill and Their Caregivers*. Boston: Wisdom, 2010.

Brounstein, Marty. *Coaching and Mentoring for Dummies*. Indianapolis: Wiley, 2000.

Cohen, Andrea S., with Leah Green and Susan Partnow. *Practicing the Art of Compassionate Listening*. Seattle: The Compassionate Listening Project, 2011. Kindle edition.

Collinson, Brian. "Water." *Vibrant Jung Thing Blog*, November 12, 2012. https://www.briancollinson.ca/index.php/2012/11/jungian-therapy-the-meaning-of-dreams-5-water.html.

Colombo, John Robert. *Neo-Poems*. Vancouver: Sono Nis, 1970.

Cordovero, Moses. *The Palm Tree of Deborah*. Translated by Moshe Miller. Southfield, MI: Targum, 1993.

Danan, Julie Hilton. "Beyond Tikkun Olam." Paper presented at Religion and Thoughtful Activism conference, Vancouver School of Theology, May 26, 2021.

Distant Prayers: COVID-10, Religion, and Conflict. Seven episodes. Produced by Isabelle Ava-Pointon for the Distant Prayers research group, Peter Wall Institute for Advanced Studies, University of British Columbia. December 23 2020. https://podcasts.apple.com/us/podcast/the-distant-prayers-pod cast/id1545482916.

Drob, Sanford. *Symbols of the Kabbalah: Philosophical and Psychological Perspectives.* Lanham, MD: Aronson, 2000.

———. "Tzimtzum: A Kabbalistic Theory of Creation." *The Jewish Review* 3.5 (1990). http://thejewishreview.org/articles/?id=121.

Dubov, Nisson Dovid. *The Sefirot.* Chabad website. https://www.chabad.org/library/article_cdo/aid/361885/jewish/The-Sefirot.htm.

Duhan-Kaplan, Laura. "The Afterlife Journey: Kabbalistic Guidelines for Death Preparation." Paper presented at "Spiritual Perspectives on Death and Dying" conference, May 23, 2018.

———. "Body and Soul: Roots of Remezim in Philo of Alexandria." *Maqom Journal of Rabbinic Literature* 3 (2002). http://www.maqom.com/journal/paper6.pdf.

———. "Educational and Philosophical Weaknesses of the Critical Thinking Movement." PhD diss., Claremont Graduate School, 1991.

———. "Healing Social Trauma: Activist Education in Graduate Study." Paper presented at "Religion and Activism" conference, Vancouver School of Theology, May 26, 2021.

———. *The Infinity Inside: Jewish Spiritual Practice through a Multi-Faith Lens.* Boulder, CO: Albion-Andalus, 2019.

———. *Mouth of the Donkey: Re-imagining Biblical Animals.* Eugene, OR: Cascade, 2021.

———. "Mysticism in Mid-Life." In *Spiritual Voices,* edited by Eleanor Clitheroe and S. Brooke Anderson, 48–55. Toronto: Thomas Merton Centre, 2018.

———. *Sophia Street Blog.* www.sophiastreet.com.

———. "A Trio of Books Applying the Ethic of Care: Personal, Institutional, and Global Dimensions." *Peace and Change* 24.4 (2000) 516–26.

———. "Vibration of the Other: A Kabbalistic Ecumenism." In *Encountering the Other: Christian and Multifaith Perspectives,* edited by Laura Duhan-Kaplan and Harry O. Maier, 118–26. Eugene, OR: Pickwick, 2020.

Finkelman, Shimon, and Yitzchak Berkowitz. *Chofetz Chaim: A Lesson a Day.* New York: Mesorah, 2008.

Firestone, Tirzah. *The Receiving: Reclaiming Jewish Women's Wisdom.* San Francisco: Harper, 2003.

———. *Wounds into Wisdom: Healing Intergenerational Jewish Trauma.* Rhinebeck, NY: Monkfish, 2019. Kindle Edition.

Gabirol, Solomon ibn. *The Fountain of Life (Fons Vitae).* Translated by Harry E. Wedeck. London: Global Grey, 2019.

Gikatilla, Joseph. *Gates of Light: Sha'are Orah.* Translated by Avi Weinstein. Lanham, MD: Altamira, 1998.

Giller, Pinchas. *Shalom Shar'abi and the Kabbalists of Beit El.* Oxford: Oxford University Press, 2008. Kindle edition.

Gordon, William J. J. *The Metaphorical Way of Learning and Knowing.* Cambridge, MA: Porpoise, 1973.

Gottlieb, Lynn. *She Who Dwells Within: A Feminist Vision of a Renewed Judaism.* New York: HarperCollins, 1995.

Green, Arthur. *Ehyeh: A Kabbalah for Tomorrow.* Woodstock, VT: Jewish Lights, 2003.

Green, Arthur, and Barry W. Holtz, trans. *Your Word Is Fire: The Hasidic Masters on Contemplative Prayer.* New York: Schocken, 1977.

Guenther, Margaret. *Holy Listening.* New York: Cowley, 1992.

Hamm, Dennis. "Rummaging for God: Praying Backwards through Your Day." *Ignatian Spirituality,* 1994. Ignatian Spirituality, https://www.ignatianspirituality.com/ignatian-prayer/the-examen/rummaging-for-god-praying-backward-through-your-day/.

Hammer, Jill. *Return to the Place: The Magic, Meditation, and Mystery of Sefer Yetzirah.* Teaneck, NJ: Ben Yehuda, 2020.

Hammer, Reuven. *Akiva: Life, Legend, Legacy.* Philadelphia: Jewish Publication Society, 2015.

Heschel, Abraham Joshua. *God in Search of Man: A Philosophy of Judaism.* New York: Farar, Straus and Giroux, 1955.

Hobbes, Thomas. *Leviathan.* New York: Penguin, 2017.

Isaacs, Ronald. "Shavuot History and Development." MyJewishLearning. https://www.myjewishlearning.com/article/shavuot-history-rabbinic-development/.

Iyengar, B. K. S. *Light on Yoga.* New York: Schocken, 1979.

Jacobi, Jolande. *Complex, Archetype, Symbol in the Psychology of C. G. Jung.* Princeton, NJ: Princeton University Press, 1959.

Jacobson, Simon. *A Spiritual Guide to the Counting of the Omer: Forty-nine Steps to Personal Refinement According to the Jewish Tradition.* New York: Meaningful Life Center, 2018. Kindle edition.

Johnson, David, and Jeff VanVonderen. *The Subtle Power of Spiritual Abuse.* Ada, MI: Baker, 1991. Kindle Edition.

Jung, C. G. *Two Essays on Analytical Psychology.* Collected Works of C. G. Jung, Volume 7. Princeton, NJ: Princeton University Press, 1967. Kindle edition.

Kimmerer, Robin Wall. *Braiding Sweetgrass.* Minneapolis: Milkweed, 2013.

Kitov, Eliyahu. *The Book of Our Heritage: The Jewish Year and Its Days of Significance.* Spring Valley, NY: Feldheim, 1997.

Kurzweil, Arthur. *Kabbalah for Dummies.* Hoboken, NJ: For Dummies, 2006.

Laërtius, Diogenes. *Lives of the Eminent Philosophers,* Translated by C. D. Yonge. London: Bell and Sons, 1915.

Lamm, Maurice. *The Jewish Way in Death and Mourning.* Middle Village, NY: David, 2000.

Leader, Ebn. "Sefirot Ha'Omer." Hebrew College blog. May 24, 2016. https://hebrewcollege.edu/blog/sefirot-haomer/.

Machon HaMidrash HaMevo'ar. *Eichah [Lamentations]: The Midrash Rabbah.* Jerusalem: Feldheim, 2004.

Maimonides, Moses. *Mishneh Torah.* Sefaria. https://www.sefaria.org/texts/ Halakhah/Mishneh%20Torah.

Matt, Daniel C., trans. *Zohar: The Pritzker Edition,* Volume 1. Stanford, CA: Stanford University Press, 2004.

Methot, Suzanne. *Legacy: Trauma, Story, and Indigenous Healing.* Toronto: ECW, 2019.

Midrash Eichah [Lamentations] Rabbah. Translated by Yaakov Blinder. Jerusalem: Feldheim, 2004.

Mir, Mustansir. *Understanding the Islamic Scripture: A Study of Selected Passages from the Qur'ān.* London: Routledge, 2016.

Morinis, Alan. *Everyday Holiness: The Jewish Spiritual Path of Musar.* Boston: Trumpeter, 2011.

Novick, Leah. *On the Wings of Shechinah: Rediscovering Judaism's Divine Feminine.* Wheaton, IL: Quest, 2008.

Otto, Rudolph. *Idea of the Holy.* Oxford: Oxford University Press, 1958.

Paley, William. *The Works of William Paley: Natural Theology.* Neuilly-sur-Seine, France: Ulan, 2012.

Pardes, Ilana. *Countertraditions in the Bible: A Feminist Approach.* Cambridge: Harvard University Press, 1992.

Philo. *On the Creation.* Translated by Charles Duke Yonge. London: Bohn, 1854. http://www.earlychristianwritings.com/yonge/book1.html.

Plato. *Phaedo.* Translated by G. M. A. Grube. Indianapolis: Hackett, 1977.

———. *Republic.* Translated by G. M. A. Grube. Indianapolis: Hackett, 1992.

———. *Symposium.* Translated by Alexander Nehemas and Paul Woodruff. Indianapolis: Hackett, 1989.

———. *The Trial and Death of Socrates: Euthyphro, Apology, Crito, Death Scene from Phaedo.* Translated by G. M. A. Grube and John M. Cooper. Indianapolis: Hackett, 2000.

Prager, Marcia. *The Path of Blessing.* Woodstock, VT: Jewish Lights, 2003.

Presler, Judith. "Weil on Power, Oppression, and Global Capitalism." In *Parceling the Globe: Philosophical Explorations in Globalization, Global Behavior, and Peace,* edited by Danielle Poe and Eddy Souffrant, 125–50. Amsterdam: Rodopi, 2008.

Prideaux, Ed. "How to Heal the Mass Trauma of COVID-19," BBC, February 3 2021. https://www.bbc.com/future/article/20210203-after-the-covid-19-pandemic-how-will-we-heal.

Raphael, Simcha Paull. *Jewish Views of the Afterlife.* Lanham, MD: Rowman and Littlefield, 2009.

Rogers, Carl. *On Becoming a Person: A Therapist's View of Psychotherapy.* New York: HarperCollins, 1995.

Rosenberg, Marshall B. *Practical Spirituality: Reflections on the Spiritual Basis of Nonviolent Communication.* Encinitas, CA: PuddleDancer, 2005.

Schachter-Shalomi, Zalman. *Jewish with Feeling: A Guide to Meaningful Jewish Practice*. Woodstock, VT: Jewish Lights, 2013.

Schneerson, Shmuel. *True Existence*. Translated by Yosef Marcus. New York: Kehot, 2002.

Schneur Zalman of Liadi. *Likutei Amarim Tanya*. New York, Kehot, 1993.

Scholem, Gershom. *Major Trends in Jewish Mysticism*. New York: Schocken, 1995. Kindle edition.

Sefer Yetzirah. Jerusalem: Yeshivat Kol Yehuda, 1990.

Segal, Michael. "Shavuot, the Festival of Covenants." TheTorah.com. https://www.thetorah.com/article/shavuot-the-festival-of-covenants.

Seigworth, Gregory, and Melissa Gregg. "An Inventory of Shimmers." In *The Affect Theory Reader*, edited by Melissa Gregg and Gregory J. Seigworth, 1–25. Durham, NC: Duke University Press, 2010. Kindle edition.

Seuss, Dr. *McElligot's Pool*. New York: Random House, 1947.

Sherwin, Byron L. *Kabbalah: An Introduction to the Jewish Mystical Tradition*. Lanham, MD: Rowman and Littlefield, 2006.

Sorensen, Roy. "Nothingness." *Stanford Encyclopedia of Philosophy*. August 31, 2017. https://plato.stanford.edu/entries/nothingness/.

Stanley, Jason. *How Fascism Works: The Politics of Us and Them*. New York: Random House, 2018.

Tishby, Isaiah. *The Wisdom of the Zohar*. London: Littman Library of Civilization, 1991.

Talbot, Thomas B. "Heaven and Hell in Christian Thought." *Stanford Encyclopedia of Philosophy*. February 20, 2021. https://plato.stanford.edu/entries/heaven-hell/.

Vital, Chayyim. *Pri Etz Chaim*. Sefaria. https://www.sefaria.org/Pri_Etz_Chaim

Waskow, Arthur. *Dancing in God's Earthquake: The Coming Transformation of Religion*. Maryknoll, NY: Orbis, 2020.

Westphal, Merold. "Immanence and Transcendence." *The Oxford Handbook of Nineteenth-Century Christian Thought*, edited by Joel D. S. Rasmussen, Judith Wolfe, and Johannes Zachhuber, 111–26. Oxford: Oxford University Press, 2017.

William Davidson Talmud. *Sefaria*. 2015. https://www.sefaria.org/texts/Talmud

Zaidi, Syed Nasir. "Belief in the Day of Judgment: Its Impact on the Development of the Human Soul." In *Visions of the End Times: Revelations of Challenge and Hope*, edited by Laura Duhan-Kaplan, Anne-Marie Ellithorpe, and Harry O. Maier. Eugene, OR: Wipf & Stock, forthcoming.

Zohar. Sefaria. https://www.sefaria.org/Zohar.

Made in United States
North Haven, CT
01 October 2023

42220359R00093